Creating Software with Modern Diagramming Techniques

Build Better Software with Mermaid

Ashley Peacock

The Pragmatic Bookshelf

Raleigh, North Carolina

Many of the designations used by manufacturers and sellers to distinguish their products are claimed as trademarks. Where those designations appear in this book, and The Pragmatic Programmers, LLC was aware of a trademark claim, the designations have been printed in initial capital letters or in all capitals. The Pragmatic Starter Kit, The Pragmatic Programmer, Pragmatic Programming, Pragmatic Bookshelf, PragProg and the linking *g* device are trademarks of The Pragmatic Programmers, LLC.

Every precaution was taken in the preparation of this book. However, the publisher assumes no responsibility for errors or omissions, or for damages that may result from the use of information (including program listings) contained herein.

For our complete catalog of hands-on, practical, and Pragmatic content for software developers, please visit *https://pragprog.com*.

The team that produced this book includes:

CEO: Dave Rankin
COO: Janet Furlow
Managing Editor: Tammy Coron
Development Editor: Michael Swaine
Copy Editor: L. Sakhi MacMillan
Layout: Gilson Graphics
Founders: Andy Hunt and Dave Thomas

For sales, volume licensing, and support, please contact *support@pragprog.com*.

For international rights, please contact *rights@pragprog.com*.

ISBN-13: 978-1-68050-983-0
Book version: P1.0—February 2023

Contents

Acknowledgments

I never thought I'd ever write a book, but I've loved every minute of writing it. I couldn't have done it alone though, so I have some awesome people to thank.

I'd like to thank the Pragmatic Bookshelf for believing in my book and vision and giving me the chance to write and publish this book. In particular, I'd like to thank my editor Michael Swaine, who has been tremendous throughout in guiding me through writing the book. Additional thanks go to Tammy Coron and Margaret Eldridge.

Furthermore, I'd like to thank my reviewers Thuan Nguyen, Adam Cox, Kelvin Samuel, and Rob Faldo, for their time and effort in helping shape the book through their feedback.

I couldn't have written this book at all without being able to practice and promote the use of diagrams at work, so for any work colleagues, past and present, thank you for being open to trying diagramming!

This book wouldn't have been possible without Mermaid. I truly believe it's a real step forward for diagramming, and it supercharges all the use cases in this book. Therefore, I want to thank each and every contributor to the library.

My girlfriend has been incredibly supportive while I write the book, thank you for your support, for taking an interest, and for listening to my many hours of book-related ramblings.

Last, but certainly not least, I'd like to thank my family for their never-ending support. In my thirty-one years on this planet, I've never felt anything besides love, support, and encouragement from my entire family, and for that I am forever grateful. Thank you for everything you've done for me; I love you all very much.

Preface

Welcome reader, and future diagram master!

Over many years, I learned the power of being able to turn words and thoughts into diagrams. I started out like most diagrammers, using a language called UML, which we'll learn all about in this book. Instantly, I saw the power a diagram could have. I'd go as far to say it's become a superpower. The ease with which you can explain something with a diagram is like nothing else, but it always felt a bit cumbersome to do with the tools that were on offer.

Then, along came Mermaid, a tool to write diagrams as you would code and automatically render them from that code. It wasn't the first to do this, but I'd argue it's the first to go mainstream and see widespread adoption and support. Suddenly, diagramming became so much more accessible. You didn't need a special program—all you needed was a text editor. Since then, I've advocated for adopting Mermaid with the companies and individuals I work with and never looked back.

Thank you for reading this book, I hope you enjoy reading it as much as I've enjoyed writing it, and hopefully you, too, will soon have the superpower of diagramming with Mermaid.

Who Should Read This Book?

This book is aimed primarily at engineers, of any level, who want to learn how to introduce diagrams into their development workflows. No prior knowledge is needed of any programming languages, and Mermaid's syntax is incredibly simple and easy to pick up. Technical concepts are mentioned in the book, such as domain-driven design, but they all have a brief introduction and explanation.

If you want to become a better engineer, and in particular become better at conveying your thoughts and ideas, then you're in the right place. There's no easier way to convey your ideas, in my opinion, than a diagram.

What's in This Book?

We'll start out by introducing most of the key concepts used throughout the book: Mermaid and UML. We'll cover a brief history of UML, get you set up with Mermaid, and even produce your first diagram!

We'll then delve into the many use cases for diagramming, including:

- Chapter 1, Document Your Domain, on page 1, where you'll be creating a domain model and we'll introduce the concept of domain-driven design to those not familiar.

- You'll learn how to easily explain different types of sequences in Chapter 3, Visualize Application and User Flows, on page 23, and Chapter 8, Visualize Code Flows, on page 87.

- Visualizing your architecture using the C4 Model in Chapter 4, Model Your Architecture, on page 37.

- Introducing diagramming to others, and ensuring your diagrams are easily accessible and up-to-date, in Chapter 10, Render Diagrams Using Native Support, on page 105, and Chapter 11, Create a Static Site with Mermaid Diagrams, on page 111.

What's Not in This Book?

While I do briefly cover key technical concepts, this book isn't going to go into deep levels of detail on anything except diagramming. For example, in Chapter 9, Design and Refactor Your Applications, on page 93, we'll touch on concepts such as classes, interfaces, and inheritance, and I do provide brief introductions to them, but you'll need to find other sources for a more in-depth understanding. In some cases, I recommend additional reading if you're interested to learn more.

How to Read This Book

The book is structured in a similar way to how I approach software development, in particular when it comes to building a new service or undertaking a new project. By no means do I always follow this order, and I regularly use diagrams ad-hoc when working on individual pieces of work or explaining concepts to colleagues. It felt like the natural order for the book, but don't feel the need to follow it exactly in order when it comes to using diagrams. Once you get into the habit of diagramming, you'll learn to see opportunities to use a diagram to improve a situation.

The code samples throughout, unless otherwise stated, are usually the full syntax for the diagram at each stage. Through each chapter, we'll build the diagram up slowly, so you can always take the markup from any given sample and render a diagram from it, or even edit it to get a feel for the language.

Online Resources

The source code for each code sample is available online at the Pragmatic Bookshelf website. Please feel free to leave feedback by submitting errata[1] entries, and you can get in touch to ask any questions or give feedback via email or Twitter.

- Email: ashley@technicalbookclub.com
- Twitter: @_ashleypeacock

Now, let's get diagramming with Mermaid!

---

1. https://devtalk.com/books/creating-software-with-modern-diagramming-techniques/errata

Introduction

Many engineers underrate the power of a diagram, both in terms of conveying their ideas and thoughts and its ability to further your career. They see drawing a diagram as a time-consuming task that requires a lot of effort. Engineers are understandably hesitant to diagram. However, I have yet to meet someone who, with a little encouragement, hasn't seen the value diagramming can bring, especially when presented with the right tools.

I've been drawing diagrams as an integral part of my job as a software engineer and architect for many years, and if it has taught me one thing, it's this:

Most engineers underrate the power of a diagram.

OK, it's taught me more than that. I've learned how useful diagrams can be in conveying my ideas and thoughts. I've learned that diagrams make me a better communicator. I've learned that diagramming has even made me a better engineer and architect because it has helped me better understand the systems I'm working on. I've learned that skill in diagramming is a career enhancer.

And I've also learned how easy it has become for anyone to develop that skill and to produce attractive, helpful diagrams in a matter of minutes.

You just need to get your hands on the right tools and some training in their use. That's what this book is for.

Using the modern diagramming tools you'll learn to master in this book, you can now create diagrams in minutes with minimal effort or technical knowledge required.

Diagramming Techniques

In this book, we'll cover two main diagramming techniques. The first is Unified Modeling Language (UML), which was first created in the mid-1990s and is now looked after by the Object Management Group, who oversee its development and updates. Its aim is to provide a standard set of diagrams to visualize the design of a system or set of systems.

UML deals with three types of diagrams: structure, behavior, and interaction. Structure diagrams represent the makeup of your systems and can be used for visualizing classes and components. Behavior diagrams model more dynamic aspects of the system and should be used to understand the behavior a system needs to handle, which is particularly useful when designing the system. Finally, interaction diagrams are used to show specific flows between processes (for example, systems), components, or classes.

They all have specific use cases, and through this book you will learn how and when to use them.

The second diagramming technique we'll use is the C4 model, which will enable us to model our software architecture in a simple and readable way.

Diagramming Tools

If you've already heard of UML, you might be thinking nothing has changed since UML was released. You've heard engineers mention it before and perhaps even seen some diagrams created using UML. The main reason I believe UML hasn't become widely used isn't because it's not a powerful tool but because the *tooling* wasn't there when it was released.

If you wanted to create a UML diagram, or any diagram, you had to find a program to use to create it, install that program, and then painstakingly draw the boxes and lines, including making sure everything lined up. As the web evolved, online UI tools that remove some of the pain appeared, but often you'd still have to spend hours drawing more complex diagrams.

Remember how I said that most engineers underrate the power of a diagram? This is why.

Why Mermaid over other tools, such as PlantUML? Some of this will become apparent in later chapters, particularly the final one, but in the past PlantUML was a hard sell to engineers as there weren't any major adoptions for it. Mermaid, however, in constrast is making waves, with GitHub and GitLab both having native support for rendering Mermaid diagrams without any additional tooling. We'll cover how this works in the last chapter, when we discuss ensuring your diagrams are kept up-to-date and easily accessible.

But times have changed, and diagramming has changed. We now have tools that eliminate the need to manually draw diagrams. Using tools like Mermaid, we can quickly and easily create an array of diagrams using syntax similar to Markdown. The majority of diagrams I created for this book, which you will see in later chapters, took no longer than ten to fifteen minutes to create the first drafts.

I think it's time for a diagramming revolution. If you look around online, you'll probably find it was over twenty years ago that the last diagramming book was released. Mermaid has arrived at the right time to rejuvenate diagramming in a new generation of engineers.

Creating Diagrams

Throughout the chapters, you'll see diagrams I've created using Mermaid, and you, too, will be creating your own diagrams. There are many ways to create diagrams using Mermaid, from the terminal to web-based tools. I'll provide a few options, so you can choose the option that you feel suits you best!

The first one is an online tool, provided by Mermaid, called Mermaid Live.[1]

It has a simple UI and will render the diagrams you define each time you edit your Mermaid markup. It has a fast feedback loop, as it will render the diagram live in the browser. It has its own bespoke code to handle the UI, so can occasionally encounter a bug or two, but generally speaking I've found it quick and easy to use. Mermaid's online editor also has several options to export diagrams as images, which saves you having to export them manually on the command line. If you prefer the command line, I'll cover that shortly.

If you want to give it a try now, here's a simple diagram to try it out:

```
flowchart LR
    a --> b & c --> d
```

It should look something like this:

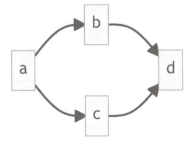

Congratulations, you created your first diagram using Mermaid!

---

1. https://mermaid.live

Mermaid Versions

 This book uses Mermaid version 9.3.0. The syntax hasn't changed since I've been using it, so all the syntax used in the book is likely to be relevant for the forseeable future.

I use this live editor regularly for throwaway diagrams—for example, quickly explaining something to a colleague, such as how a particular flow works or a set of classes work together.

If you prefer to use your own editor of choice, Mermaid is supported in sevaral editors. VS Code has its own plugin, as does Sublime. Similarly, Vim has a Mermaid package available. Mermaid's GitHub repository has the full list of supported editor integration.[2]

It's naturally down to personal preference, but I've found "Markdown Preview Mermaid Support" for VS Code to be the best editor plugin so far.[3] It works well and allows you to see how your diagram is being rendered in real time.

Using the Command Line

If you prefer to use the command line to export images out of Mermaid, you're in luck—Mermaid has its own CLI!

Detailed installation instructions are available on the Mermaid CLI repo, available at https://github.com/mermaid-js/mermaid-cli. Once installed, you can check everything is working by creating a file containing the following Mermaid code:

```
flowchart LR
    a --> b & c--> d
```

Once created, you can run the following command:

```
mmdc -i path-to-your-mermaid-file.mmd -o output.png
```

This will ingest the Mermaid markup and generate a PNG in the same directory. Mermaid also supports generating SVG and PDF, if you prefer those formats. If you would rather avoid installing dependencies such as Node and Yarn on your machine, a pre-built Docker image is available to use, which is documented in the GitHub repo too.

---

2.   https://github.com/mermaid-js/mermaid/blob/develop/docs/integrations.md#editor-plugins
3.   https://marketplace.visualstudio.com/items?itemName=bierner.markdown-mermaid

Please do reach out if you get stuck at any point in the book or have any questions!

Now that you're all set up with your workflow of choice, we can move on to the really fun stuff!

In the course of this book, we'll look at tools and techniques to enable you to bring your diagrams to life and ensure they have longevity, and don't simply become static images that are forgotten about or that people can't update. Not being able to quickly and easily update and publish diagrams is another reason I believe engineers have been apprehensive to use them. We're going to make that problem go away with some simple techniques you'll learn in the following pages.

Document Your Domain

In the following chapters, we're going to go through the life cycle of creating an application from scratch. We won't be writing any application code, but we will be documenting the important steps with diagrams. I've written the chapters roughly in the order I would go about each step in my professional career, but you may find a slightly different order works for you.

To start off, we're going to create a domain model. Domain modeling is the primary way of determining the important aspects of a business. It's usually created collaboratively by engineering, product, and business stakeholders to ensure all major parts of the business are aligned on what the domain model looks like.

That makes it a good candidate for diagramming. By documenting your domain models with a diagram, that domain model is going to come to life and is more likely to be practiced. Furthermore, due to the ease of Mermaid, it's possible to create a draft of the domain model in real time when discussing with colleagues in a meeting.

I recommend reading *Domain-Driven Design: Tackling Complexity in the Heart of Software [Eva03]* if you're keen to learn more about DDD.

Once you've got to grips with domain modeling, it's going to make your life so much easier. There will be moments during domain modeling where suddenly it all comes together, everyone is on the same page in terms of their understanding of the landscape, and everyone is speaking the same language.

The most powerful use of DDD I've experienced was working for an insurance company. The team I was working in had been tasked with creating a way to determine how exactly our products were sold and to whom—sounds easy, right? Unfortunately, the data was all over the place, and customers could use many avenues to make a purchase, with varying data available in each avenue. None of us had any idea how to represent these conceptions in our code, so we spent several days domain modeling. We tried out different ideas and approaches, and in the end we landed on a culmination of a few different ideas and were able to easily translate the domain model into code.

I find the biggest power that comes from domain modeling is the collaboration, how it brings everyone on the journey and ultimately to the same destination. It becomes easy to talk about what we are working on, as we're all speaking the same language, and the code flows easily because we have a clear idea of how we should represent these business requirements using our domain model. By the end of the project, even nontechnical stakeholders were using the same terminology that we had come up with while domain modeling.

The final selling point I'll make for DDD is its ability to allow your domain and code to evolve over time. Because we're documenting our domain model, we can reference it at any point. It's very common for new requirements to come along later, at which point we can refer back to the domain model, see if it fits the new requirements, and if not, it can evolve and adjust as necessary. The core of the domain we modeled at the insurance company is still intact today but has since evolved to add new entities and use cases.

Within UML, one type of diagram available to us is called a class diagram. It can be used to model classes, but it can also be used to model domains, which makes a lot of sense when you consider your domain model is implemented in your codebase with classes. The real power of the diagram is realized when we start to model relationships between entities, which we can easily do with a UML class diagram.

Determine the Important Entities

Firstly, when creating your domain model, think of all the important entities within your business. For those unfamiliar with the term, an entity represents a core concept within the business. Entities are typically the phrases that are most used in the codebase and in meetings. A book publisher, for example, would likely have entities such as book, chapter, and author. We won't be going to this level of detail, but in your codebase they would contain entity data and business logic. Continuing the publishing example, a book would have a title for data and perhaps some business logic that calculates the word count.

The fictional company I'll be using through these chapters is called Streamy, which is trying to make a name for itself in the video streaming industry.

I would say for a video streaming company, its most important entity is likely to be Title—representing the actual videos Streamy offers their customers.

Once you've thought of an entity, what related entities might you have?

Typically, each Title will belong to a Genre, and each Genre will have a list of Titles associated with it. We've now identified two entities and how those two entities are related to one another, so we can start to form our domain model next.

> ### Domain-Driven Design
>
> Alongside domain modeling sits domain-driven design (DDD), which is a methodology not only for determining the domain model but keeping that domain model alive in the codebases you work on by ensuring the entities in your domain model are represented in your codebase.
>
> If you're not familiar with either construct, I highly recommend reading about them after reading this book, but even without knowing DDD in depth, you can have a go at creating a domain model later in the chapter.

Document Our First Relationship

Now that we understand what domain-driven design is and what it's used for, we can begin to create a domain model for Streamy.

We're going to use Mermaid to create our domain model, and adding these two entities is super-simple:

```
classDiagram
    Title -- Genre
```

That's it—our first two entities are defined! If we generate the diagram, it looks like this:

In Mermaid, the markup for any diagram (with the exception of adjusting configuration, which we will cover later) is the type of diagram you wish to create. In our case, that's a classDiagram, which informs Mermaid how to format and interpret the following lines.

When creating a domain model in UML, each line after the initial line documents a relationship between two entities. In the case of Title and Genre, where each entity is going to hold a reference to the other, that type of relationship is known as an *association*. In Mermaid, that's where the second line comes in:

```
Title -- Genre
```

To define any relationship, we write down the two entities separated by a set of symbols that define the type of relationship. An association is defined using two hyphens. Let's look at associations in more detail.

Define Associations

Association is the first type of relationship we'll cover, and it's the loosest type of relationship available within a UML class diagram. Usually, for a relationship to be classed as an association, the entities must be able to exist independently of one another and likely have their own life cycles. Furthermore, there is generally no "owner" of the relationship for associations, they're simply linked. In that way, you can think of their relationship as "using" one another rather than one owning the other.

In our case of Title and Genre, we could have a page on our application that just shows Genres without any Titles. However, we probably want to be able to list the Titles within a Genre, and display a specific Title's Genre too, so they need to have a link of some sort, as all relationships must be documented in a domain model.

Associations are very loose ways to link two entities, but some relationships form a closer bond between two entities. Let's look at one next.

Define Composite Relationships

Once you have your first two entities defined, think of other entities that relate to either of them. We're going to focus on Title, as that's our main entity. I can think of two related entities:

- Season
- Review

These two entities don't suit an association, though. Similarly to associations, we have to think about how each of these behave in relation to Title. They don't make sense on their own like an association, and without Title, they probably make no sense at all in our domain. After all, if we deleted Title, it would be impossible to have either of these exist. For example, you can't have a Season for a nonexistent Title, and the same is true for Review.

This type of relationship is called *composition*, and we can document it as follows in Mermaid, using an asterisk and two hyphens:

```
classDiagram
    Title -- Genre
    Title *-- Season
    Title *-- Review
```

And if we generate the diagram, it looks like so:

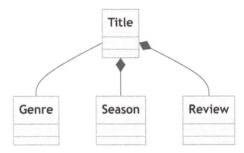

Notice the difference between the different classes. Title and Genre are linked via a solid line with no arrows, whereas Title and Season have a solid diamond on the line connecting them, which signifies the relationship is composition.

The side the diamond is on indicates the class holding the reference, but you can think of it similarly to a parent and child relationship, where the diamond signifies the parent, as the child cannot exist without the parent. Unlike associations, the parent is the owner of the relationship.

Relationship Direction

While Mermaid will allow you to write the relationships in either direction (for example, '*–' and '–*'), I recommend always putting the parent on the left for easier readability and less cognitive load of working out the direction of the relationship, as you can just read from left to right.

To complete the composite relationships we need for our domain model, a Season isn't much use without its counterpart Episode. Much like our other composite relationships, an Episode *probably* doesn't make much sense without belonging to a Season. Once adding our final composite relationship, our Mermaid code looks like so:

```
classDiagram
    Title -- Genre
    Title *-- Season
    Title *-- Review

    Season *-- Episode
```

While the layout is totally up to you and personal preference, I prefer to group each entity's relationships together and separate the groups with an empty line to aid readability.

> ### DDD Is Opinionated
>
> Domain-driven design is very opinionated, so keep in mind you might not model my examples like this if you were creating them. The model itself isn't the important part, at least in the context of this book—the syntax and the diagrams themselves are.

We now know two relationship types:

- *Associations*, which are two entities that are loosely related and can exist independent of one another.

- *Compositions*, which indicate two entities are tightly related and cannot exist independently of one another.

One more, though, sits between those two in terms of how closely related two entities are. We'll cover that in the next section.

Define Aggregate Relationships

Our domain model is starting to take form, but it's still missing a few key entities. After all, doesn't everyone like to know the Actors that appear in a Title?

But this entity doesn't suit a composite relationship. While knowing the Actors is definitely handy, Title could exist without Actors, and similarly an Actor can exist independently of a Title (or belong to many Titles, so if one was deleted, they'd perhaps exist on another, so would remain in place).

Let's update our Mermaid code to add Actor:

```
classDiagram
    Title -- Genre
    Title *-- Season
    Title *-- Review
    Title o-- Actor

    Season *-- Episode
```

The syntax for *aggregate* relationships is o-- (the letter o followed by two hyphens), and once generated this is how they are rendered:

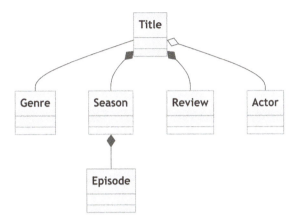

An aggregate relationship is also displayed as a diamond, but instead of being a solid diamond, it's empty. In an aggregate relationship, there's still an owner—the parent. However, the bond between them isn't as strong as a composite relationship, and if the parent were to be deleted, the child can still exist.

As mentioned at the start of the chapter, choices of how to model a domain can vary greatly between companies or colleagues. In another domain model, perhaps you group Actors into a Cast for example. That would change the type of relationship, perhaps, to a composite relationship, as a Cast created for a Title probably wouldn't remain if the Title were deleted.

Now that we know the main three types of relationship we can use, let's consider when to use each one.

Decide Between Association, Aggregation, and Composition

We've covered the three main types of relationship we can use when domain modeling, but when should you use each one?

It can be difficult at times to work out which type of relationship best reflects entities' real-world interaction, and often opinions will differ between colleagues. If you ask two different sets of people to model the same domain, they would almost certainly come up with not only different names for the entities but different relationships. One of the main benefits of domain modeling is that it aligns everyone to the same constructs, and as everyone is working for the same company, there's no real "right" and "wrong," as it's all based on mutual understanding.

As for working out the right type of relationship, I tend to follow this guidance:

- *Association*: there's a relationship between the entities, with at least one entity holding a reference to the other. There's no owner of the relationship though, and they can exist completely independently of one another. An example separate from Streamy might be a Teacher and Student relationship.

- *Aggregations*: there's a more direct relationship between the entities than an association, but they can still exist independently of one another. There's an owner of the relationship, but if the parent is deleted, the child can still remain. Continuing the education theme, a Teacher has an aggregate relationship to Class. You could delete the Teacher, but the Class would still remain and make sense on its own.

- *Compositions*: the closest of relationships is reserved for compositions. Similarly to aggregations, there's an owner of the relationship. However, if the parent is deleted, the child must be deleted, too, and makes no sense without its parent relationship. Picking up the education theme once more, Grade could be a composite relation to Class—if the Class were deleted, the Grade probably wouldn't make sense unless it's linked to a Class.

That's it for the first chapter on documenting a domain model. We'll cover more aspects to documenting a domain in the next chapter. For now though, it's time for you to create a domain model diagram!

Document Your Own Domain

It's your turn to put what you've learned into practice. Most chapters from now onward will suggest at least one exercise for you to complete to learn each diagram we cover.

For this chapter, create your own domain model using what you've learned so far. In the following chapter, we'll enhance our domain model with more features and techniques.

I recommend one of the following options:

- You can use a fictional company as I have done.

- Pick a well-known company that you know well enough to model.

- Use a company you've worked for prior who didn't have a documented domain model.

- Model a side project or future project you want to work on.

Each chapter will build on the previous ones, so I recommend sticking with whatever company you pick throughout the chapters. Similarly to Streamy, you do not need to model the entire domain—there is a lot more to add if Streamy were a real company—but aim to add at least seven entities.

Your goal for this chapter is to be able to create a domain model using what we've covered.

What You've Learned

Congratulations, you've made your first Mermaid diagram! Let's recap what you've learned in this chapter:

Domain modeling is the primary way of determining the important aspects of a business, and domain-driven design is the methodology used to bring that domain model to life in your day-to-day work. We start by identifying the core entities within our domain. We can keep modeling our domain until all the key entities are represented in our domain model.

For each entity, we add a node to our UML class diagram and define the relationships between them. Relationships should be defined between the entities and can be of types assocation, composite, or aggregate.

Now that we have the core of our domain model defined, we can start adding more advanced aspects to our domain model. In the next chapter, we'll cover a little about Mermaid's rendering and how we can influence it, and we'll add more detailed information to the relationships in our domain model.

CHAPTER 2

Enhance Your Domain Model

In the prior chapter, we covered the basics of domain modeling and the basics of how to create a domain model with Mermaid. There's much more to learn though, particularly in how we can enhance the domain model with more rich information.

In this chapter, you'll learn how to show inheritance in order to show subtypes and how to provide more information to anyone viewing the diagram with descriptions and something called multiplicity.

The folks at Streamy are eager to get their product to market, so let's dive right in and complete their domain model!

Define Inheritance

Besides association, aggregation, and composition from the last chapter, we have a way to show inheritence within our domain model.

Title is an abstract term deliberately—after all Streamy wants to offer a range of video content to its prospective customers. To start off with, we want to offer TV Show, Film, and Short. In object-oriented programming, these might be represented as subclasses of Title.

We can reflect that within UML using a generalization.

Let's add that to our existing Mermaid code:

```
classDiagram
    Title -- Genre
    Title *-- Season
    Title *-- Review
    Title o-- Actor
```

```
TV Show --|> Title
Short --|> Title
Film --|> Title

Season *-- Episode
```

Generalizations are defined using --|>, and will be represented on the rendered diagram as an arrow. If you're familiar with UML, they're typically shown as empty arrows, but in Mermaid they're solid arrows.

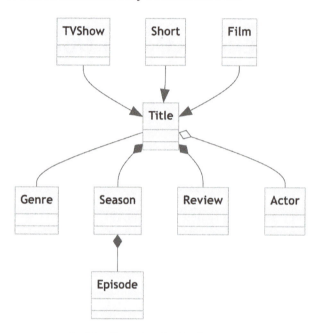

Generalizations are probably the simplest of associations as they are more familiar and easily recognizable to anyone who's worked with inheritance in programming, and they behave in exactly the same way. Another example might be the entities Dog and Cat, which have the generalization Animal.

You may have noticed TV Show has had its space removed, which is a quirk of using a class diagram for a domain model, as class names in code never contain spaces. Hopefully in the future spaces are supported, but for now I think it's not major and the important information is still conveyed well.

As we've now added a number of entities and relationships to our domain model, let's take a closer look at what Mermaid does for us in terms of rendering.

Mermaid's Powerful Rendering

It's possible, and very common, for diagrams to become complex—especially domain models. If you've ever had to create any form of diagram manually, you'll know the pain of adding in a new box and drawing the arrows. If you haven't, consider yourself lucky! It can be painstakingly slow to create diagrams by hand, and when you're taking part in domain modeling, it's likely the model will evolve rapidly. All of a sudden, you might have a need to insert an entity right in the middle. With a manually drawn diagram, this would be a nightmare, especially while screen sharing!

However, with Mermaid this is all handled for you by the library. Do you need to insert an entity right in the middle? Simply add it, and Mermaid will instantly re-render the diagram in the most readable way possible.

We're going to extend the relationship for Review, as realistically a Review can be left for a Title, Season or Episode.

Here are all our entities represented on the domain model:

```
classDiagram
    Title -- Genre
    Title *-- Season
    Title *-- Review
    Title o-- Actor

    TV Show --|> Title
    Short --|> Title
    Film --|> Title

    Season *-- Review
    Season *-- Episode

    Episode *-- Review
```

Now comment out each Review relation (from bottom to top) in the Mermaid code and generate the diagram after adding each one, and note how Mermaid reshuffles the diagram to make it as readable as possible. Comments in Mermaid are made using %% at the start of the line (for example, %% Episode *-- Review).

This is one of the huge benefits of Mermaid versus more manual tools—it allows for rapid iteration over a domain model. You could feasibly completely rewrite the model in a short amount of time without tediously redrawing numerous arrows and labels. This is especially useful for domain modeling, where you may want to try out ideas visually when discussing the domain model with colleagues and quickly change tact if needed.

Hopefully you can now see how powerful Mermaid is, especially over manual tools that put you in charge of the layout. We can now begin to enrich the domain model with more information, starting with adding descriptions to relationships.

Describe Relationships

One of the key features of a domain model written with UML is that you can, and should, describe how the entities interact with regard to their relationships. In a lot of cases, and in the case of our domain model we have so far, a lot of the descriptions can be simply described as has. Be as descriptive as possible, and try to avoid using has for everything where possible.

More detailed descriptions for relationships come into play when the actors are added to a model (for example, customers or viewers). I've added descriptions to each relationship and updated the Mermaid code:

```
classDiagram
    Title -- Genre: is associated with
    Title *-- Season: has
    Title *-- Review: has
    Title o-- Actor: features

    TV Show --|> Title: implements
    Short --|> Title: implements
    Film --|> Title: implements

    Viewer --> Title: watches

    Season *-- Review: has
    Season *-- Episode: contains

    Episode *-- Review: has
```

I added in a Viewer entity that watches Titles to demonstrate a more descriptive label, which also shows how to add directional association using --> instead of simply two hyphens (which demonstrated bidirectional association, as we saw earlier with Genre and Title). This means Viewer holds a reference to Title, but Title doesn't hold a reference to Viewer. This makes a lot of sense, as a Viewer can naturally watch Titles, but the same cannot be said in reverse—unlike Genre and Title, where they can both reasonably hold references to one another.

For descriptions that are bidirectional, such as Title and Genre, we must describe it in a way that it works for both. In our example, a Title is associated with a Genre (and vice versa).

Lastly, for the generalizations, I've chosen to describe them using implements. All this is doing is making clear that Title is a generalization, and it has specializations such as Film and Short. It has strong links to inheritance in programming, so implements or extends are both fine. The only reason I include anything at all is to convey to those not familiar with the diagram's arrows that this is an inheritance relationship, where Title has different types.

For all the other relationships, the description is written from the parent's point of view (for example, Season contains Episodes).

Mermaid is intuitive, so adding descriptions to relationships is achieved by simply adding a colon to the end of the line you want to describe and then writing your description.

Once generated, it looks like this:

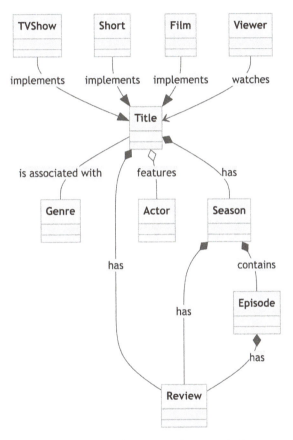

Anyone reading the domain model now understands how two entities relate to each other thanks to the descriptions we just added. But how do you know the number of entities that can relate to one another? For example, is there one A related to B, or are there many? We'll cover this next by taking a look in detail at what's called multiplicity.

Add Multiplicity

Our domain model is almost complete, with just a couple of final touches to go. We've added our entities, linked them via relationships, and described the way in which they are related. However, one thing we're missing is how many of one type of entity relates to another. This is called *multiplicity*, and it sounds complicated, but you'll soon see it's not. You've likely encountered using language like this before, especially if you've worked with relational databases.

You may have noticed that when we write our entities, they're always written in the singular form. This is again a nod to the fact that our code, which will use singular names in class names, should reflect our domain model. Furthermore, it might be possible, such as the case of Title and Season, that some Titles might contain a single Season, but others might contain multiple Seasons.

If we always named the entities as plural to account for these cases, it would be easy for readers of the diagram to misunderstand and assume there are always multiple, even if that's not the case.

Luckily, we can define what's called multiplicity on our domain model. A fancy term, but in essence it allows you to define whether the relationships are one-to-one, one-to-many, none-to-many, many-to-many, and everything in between (for example, more unusual ones such as two-to-three).

Let's add multiplicity to our Mermaid code:

```
classDiagram
    Title "1..*" -- "1..*" Genre: is associated with

    Title "1" *-- "0..*" Season: has
    Title "1" *-- "0..*" Review: has
    Title "0..*" o--  "1..*" Actor: has

    TV Show --|> Title: implements
    Short --|> Title: implements
    Film --|> Title: implements

    Viewer "0..*" --> "0..*" Title: watches

    Season "1" *-- "0..*" Review: has
    Season "1" *-- "1..*" Episode: has

    Episode "1" *-- "0..*" Review: has
```

Once rendered, it looks like the diagram shown on page 17.

Multiplicity Rendering in Safari

At the time of writing, a bug in Safari on MacOS prevents the multiplicity to render. There's an open issue being looked at, but for now, I recommend using a different browser for creating Mermaid diagrams if you're using mermaid.live.

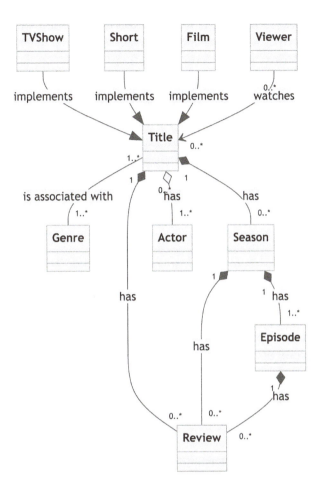

To define multiplicity on each relationship, we can optionally put them either side of the relationship identifier (for example, -- in the first line). I initially found the way these are defined a little odd, as they feel like they're on the wrong side when reading. Collectively they're known as multiplicity, and within a relationship's multiplicity each side is known as a single entity's *cardinality*.

To explain what I mean, let's look at Title and Season. Its line looks like so:

```
Title "1" *-- "0..*" Season: has
```

If we translate this into English, it would read as follows:

- Title has zero to many Seasons.
- Season belongs to one Title.

However, if you were reading it from left to right as the code shows it, you would *probably* read it as "Title has 1 Season," as that's the first cardinality you get to. An entity's cardinality is defined on the opposite side of the relationship, which can be confusing to begin with.

To help remember how cardinality is defined, particularly when I am looking at past diagrams, I find it helps to mentally "skip" the first cardinality you get to. So in the example of Title and Season, when reading Title's cardinality, you ignore the 1 and read the rest (Title has 0 to many Seasons). The ordering is slightly off as the label is at the end, but it's the best way I've found of quickly understanding at a glance. This works whether you're reading from left to right or right to left.

You might be wondering why I chose 0-to-many and not 1-to-many for Seasons—it was simply because it's possible to have a title without any seasons yet (for example, it just has a trailer, with a coming soon notice for the seasons).

Add a Title

One of the first tips I picked up when learning how to diagram was to always add a title to your diagram. It bleeds over from charts, I imagine, where a chart without a title can often be misinterpreted.

Luckily, Mermaid added title support for all diagrams as of version 9.3.0. For me, this was a much-needed feature, and I'm incredibly grateful it's been added.

We can add a title to any Mermaid diagram simply by adding the following block of code to the top of the markup. It must go at the very top, even above the diagram type definition. As we're currently working with a class diagram, the top of our diagram markup would look like this:

```
---
title: Streamy Domain Model
---
classDiagram
```

Improve Readability

As we covered earlier in Mermaid's Powerful Rendering, on page 12, Mermaid is deciding how to render the diagram, but it doesn't always get it perfect. The rendering is being improved with each version, and in the case of class diagrams, a new renderer is currently being worked on.

For the moment, however, we don't have too much control over the layout. You can change the order of statements in your Mermaid code to potentially alter the display of each node, but in some cases this won't work, as Mermaid under the covers has a particular method for rendering diagrams.

In the case of our diagram, a lot is linked to Title. It would benefit from being a little larger, and we can control the style via CSS, but this is only supported if you render the diagrams yourself on your own website—something that you won't often be doing. Work is planned to allow styling from within the markup itself for class diagrams, at which point having more control over the rendering will be possible.

For now, though, we can make a box a little bigger height-wise by adding the following anywhere after the first time Title is used:

```
%% Added to improve readability
Title: \n\n
```

Essentially, because we're using a class diagram, there will be two small empty boxes below the title, which in a class diagram would be populated with its properties and methods (you'll be learning about those in Chapter 8, Visualize Code Flows, on page 87). Those fields are irrelevant in a domain model, so we don't fill them in, but we can make use of their space using a new line, which helps space out the lines a bit, as shown in the diagram on page 20.

It's certainly not perfect, but ultimately we're sacrificing some style points for a maintainable, updatable diagram—a reasonable trade-off.

Enrich Nodes with Links

Our domain model is now finished, but I want to show you one more bit of Mermaid magic: how to link your nodes to web pages.

Each node in the diagram can have a link related to it that makes it clickable. This can be useful to link to documentation on that entity if it sits separately to the diagram, as an example.

Nodes can have links added to them by using the following:

```
link Title "http://www.example.com" _blank
```

link tells Mermaid we want to create the link, Title is the identifier of the node, followed by the URL, and, finally, the setting for how the link is opened (for example, same window or a new window).

It's possible to call custom JavaScript code using a similar syntax, but it will become apparent when you get to Render Mermaid Within Markdown Files, on page 106, why we aren't going to be using that.

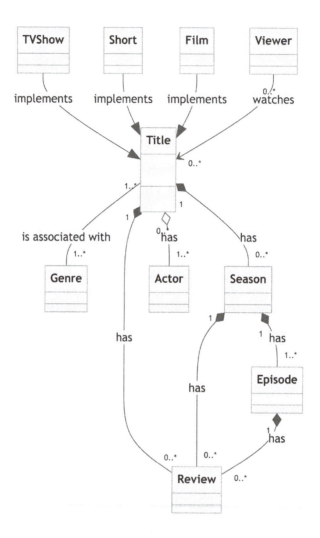

Enhance Your Domain Model

In the last chapter, we created the core of our domain model, which should have contained the majority of the entities. For this chapter, we'll continue working on that domain model and add the following:

- If applicable to your domain, add some generalizations to show inheritance. Even if it's not perfect for your domain, try adding it in briefly so you get the syntax down.

- Add descriptions to all the relationships.

- Define multiplicity for all the relationships.

- Have a go at adjusting the size of some of the nodes, using what you learned in Improve Readability, on page 18.

- Create a link to an external page (it can be any page) and try clicking it.

Once you've completed all the points, you've created an entire domain model, with all the bells and whistles!

What You've Learned

Excellent work so far—creating an entire domain model is no mean feat. Let's recap what you've learned in this chapter:

Domain modeling is the primary way of determining the important aspects of a business, and domain-driven design is the methodology used to bring that domain model to life in your day-to-day work. We start by identifying the core entities within our domain. We can keep modeling our domain until all the key entities are represented in our domain model.

For each entity, we add a node to our UML class diagram and define the relationships between them. Relationships should be defined between the entities and can be of types assocation, composite, aggregate, or generalization. Finally, we can define the multiplicity (one-to-one, one-to-many, and so on) between the entities.

Now that we have our domain model defined, we can start thinking about the interactions between different services and how we model those. In the next chapter, you'll learn how to understand and visualize the flows within your applications.

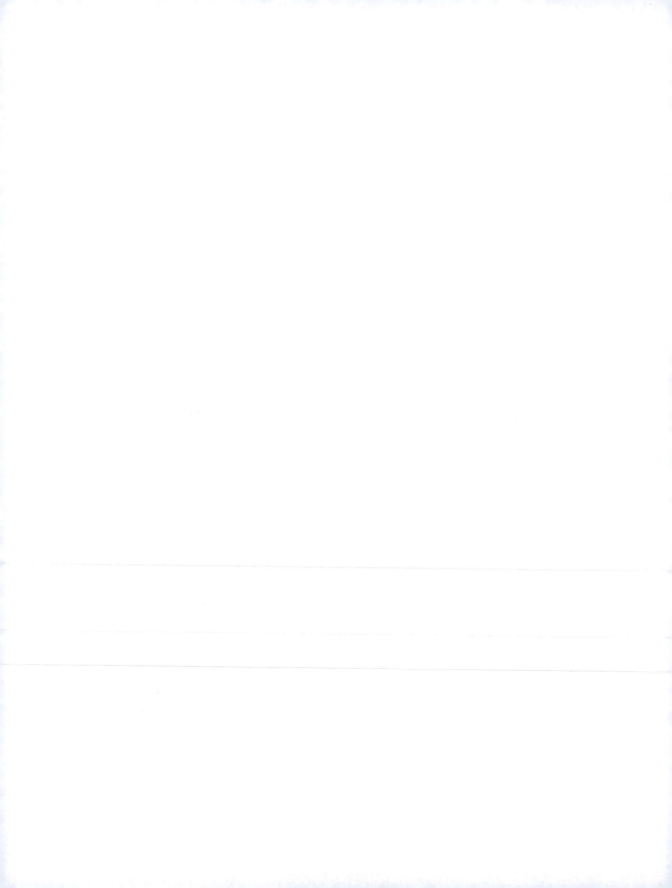

## CHAPTER 3

Visualize Application and User Flows

In the last chapter, you learned about domain modeling and should now have a finished domain model. In this chapter, we're going to look at how we can create diagrams to understand the flows you'll be using between different systems. I find it useful at the start of projects to diagram the high-level interactions I'm aiming for between systems before getting into the nitty-gritty.

Furthermore, these high-level interactions can be discussed with nontechnical colleagues to ensure what you're planning on building actually fulfils the criteria of the project. That's another benefit to this approach: we can use them to explain the flow we're expecting to build to other engineers or even nontechnical colleagues, such as product managers.

Leaning into UML once more, we can leverage a sequence diagram for this use case. A common use case I've found sequence diagrams to excel at is when getting approval to build a brand-new system. In most companies, this will need to be approved by an architect or group of architects and involves some form of documentation, and likely a presentation. I've attended the approval meeting many times, and you can see the struggle people have understanding the interactions between this new system and the existing systems when faced with just a wall of text.

When I had to present a proposal for a new system at this meeting, my document was supplemented by sequence diagrams. Others in the company would complain that they struggled to get their ideas across or it was hard to get an approval, but my experience was different. I didn't even use much of the text in the document; I simply presented the sequence diagrams (along with Using the C4 Model, on page 38), and everyone found it very easy to understand what I was proposing. Ultimately I received approvals relatively quickly.

This isn't just the case for sequence diagrams—almost any time you're presenting something, consider whether a diagram would be a better way to explain it, rather than words on a slide or talking at people without any visual aids.

We'll once again lean on UML to model our application flows, this time leveraging sequence diagrams. Once again, we can use Mermaid to allow us to quickly and easily create the diagram. A real-world application will have many flows, but our sequence diagram is going to model the flow for a user signing up for Streamy. Let's get started!

Define Actors and Participants

All sequence diagrams must have actors and participants. An actor represents a human, and a participant represents a process (for example, a service or database that runs in a UNIX process). To account for actors and participants, you should start every sequence like this:

```
---
title: User Sign Up Flow
---
sequenceDiagram
    actor Browser
    participant Sign Up Service
    participant User Service
    participant Kafka
```

As with all Mermaid diagrams, the first line defines the type of diagram we're creating. On the second line, we define a title for our diagram—we should aim to add a title to every diagram where possible.

On the remaining lines, we define the nodes in the sequence (called lifelines in UML). The browser is operated by a human, so I find it easier to mark that as an actor, and the rest are systems of some sort.

If we generate the diagram, it will look like this:

As there are no lines yet, it looks a little strange, but it does show the key nodes in this particular business process.

> ### Actors and Participants Are Optional
>
> You don't need to explicitly define the actors and participants; you could simply draw the interactions (as we will shortly) and omit them from the top of the definition. However, to display a node as a stick figure, you must explicitly define that node as an actor.
>
> Secondly, you can define aliases for participants, like this for example:
>
> ```
> participant SUS as Sign Up Service
> ```
>
> When defining messages between participants, you can then use the shorter alias rather than its full name, which will still be rendered on the diagram.
>
> There's one more reason to explicitly define them, which I will cover later.

Add Our First Interaction

Now that we've defined the actors and participants, we can start detailing the interactions between them. The first interaction, which kicks off the sign up flow, is the user requesting the sign up page—so let's add that to our sequence diagram:

```
---
title: User Sign Up Flow
---
sequenceDiagram
    actor Browser
    participant Sign Up Service
    participant User Service
    participant Kafka

    Browser->>Sign Up Service: GET /sign_up
    Sign Up Service-->>Browser: 200 OK (HTML page)
```

In sequence diagrams, interactions between nodes are modeled in the form of messages. In our first interaction, there are two messages: the first one from the browser to the sign up service to request the page, and the response from the service containing the HTML for the browser to render. If we render this definition, it looks like the diagram shown on page 26.

Messages can be added in a variety of formats, and we'll cover more later, but for now we want to use ->> for synchronous calls, which will show a solid line with a solid arrowhead. For reply messages, we use -->> which will show

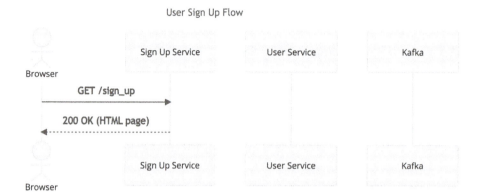

a dotted line with a solid arrowhead. This allows the reader to easily distinguish between requests and responses.

The node sending the message goes on the left of the arrow, and the node receiving the messages goes on the right.

Finally, each message should be labeled with a brief description.

Remember!

 Sequence diagrams are high-level views of a process, so try to keep the labels high-level too.

We've now added our first interaction, but most sequence diagrams are usually made up of more complex interactions than just lines back and forth. That's where the ability to define branching logic comes in.

Show Branching Logic

The majority of flows will at least have a happy path and an unhappy path. The happy path is where everything goes perfectly (for example, the user is able to register first time), and an example of an unhappy path (there are usually several) might be the user validation fails on the first submission.

Steer clear of detailing *everything* that could go wrong for every unhappy path, otherwise the sequence diagram is going to become hard to understand, but detailing a few major elements of an unhappy path is helpful to identify the major area on which error handling should be focused.

If you want to model more unhappy paths, create separate sequence diagrams for each one to keep them readable.

Using the preceding example for a user failing validation checks, here's how we can detail one of the unhappy paths in our flow and also the happy path:

```
---
title: User Sign Up Flow
---
sequenceDiagram
    actor Browser
    participant Sign Up Service
    participant User Service
    participant Kafka

    Browser->>Sign Up Service: GET /sign_up
    Sign Up Service-->>Browser: 200 OK (HTML page)

    Browser->>Sign Up Service: POST /sign_up
    Sign Up Service->>Sign Up Service: Validate input

    alt invalid input
        Sign Up Service-->>Browser: Error
    else valid input
        Sign Up Service->>User Service: POST /users
        User Service-->>Sign Up Service: 201 Created (User)
        Sign Up Service-->>Browser: 301 Redirect (Login page)
    end
```

Better Readability with Spacing

This is entirely down to personal preference, but I always find it aids readability to separate distinct sections in the diagram definition with an empty line. In sequence diagrams, I always put a space between a set of messages finishing and another starting, such as in this example.

It won't make any difference to the rendered diagram, but it will make it a little more readable for others to edit in the future.

When rendered, it will look like the diagram shown on page 28.

Let's break it down line by line:

```
Browser->>Sign Up Service: POST /sign_up
```

Firstly, we define another synchronous message from the browser to the sign up service.

```
alt invalid input
    Sign Up Service->>Browser: Error
```

Secondly, we define the first branch of our logic. Branching logic, known as alternative paths in Mermaid, look exactly like conditional statements from

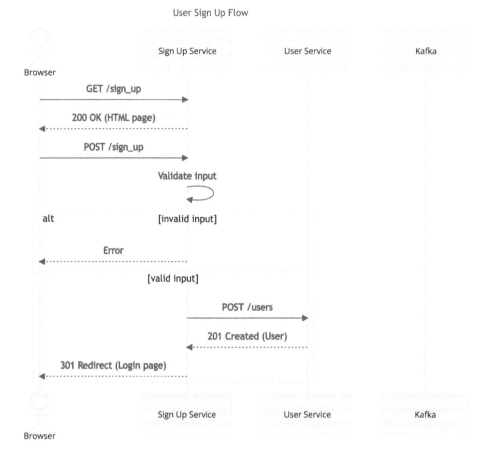

conventional programming languages. In our first branch, we return an error to the browser if the validation fails.

```
else valid input
    Sign Up Service->>User Service: POST /users
    User Service-->>Sign Up Service: 201 Created (User)
    Sign Up Service-->>Browser: 301 Redirect (Login page)
end
```

Finally, we can define the other half of the branch—the happy path. In the happy path, we define an extra synchronous call with its respective response from the user service, and then the sign up service issues a 301 redirect to the browser so the user is prompted to log in using their newly created account.

Our sequence diagram is starting to take shape and now allows the viewer of the diagram to understand the complexity in the flow. We've only added synchronous messages so far, but what about messages that are sent asynchronously?

> ### Defining Multiple Alternate Paths
>
> You can define multiple else statements if you wish to handle more than two branches, like this for example:
>
> alt-paths.txt
> ```
> alt first case
>     A->>B: first case
> else second case
>     A->>C: second case
> else third case
>     A->>D: third case
> end
> ```
>
> I recommend keeping them to a minimum though; otherwise readability will be impacted.

Display Asynchronous Messages

So far, our sequence diagram only has synchronous messages in the form of HTTP requests/responses. It's common in today's world to leverage asynchronous messaging. With Streamy having big ambitions, they probably want to make use of asynchronous communication. We can easily define asynchronous interactions with Mermaid. We're going to add an asynchronous message as part of the user creation process, which looks like this:

```
---
title: User Sign Up Flow
---
sequenceDiagram

    actor Browser
    participant Sign Up Service
    participant User Service
    participant Kafka

    Browser->>Sign Up Service: GET /sign_up
    Sign Up Service-->>Browser: 200 OK (HTML page)

    Browser->>Sign Up Service: POST /sign_up
    Sign Up Service->>Sign Up Service: Validate input

    alt invalid input
        Sign Up Service-->>Browser: Error
    else valid input
        Sign Up Service->>User Service: POST /users
        User Service--)Kafka: User Created Event Published
        User Service-->>Sign Up Service: 201 Created (User)
        Sign Up Service-->>Browser: 301 Redirect (Login page)
    end
```

In the else statement we've simply added one message from the user service to Kafka, which will be a user-created domain event. Asynchronous messages are defined using --), which will render a dotted line with an empty arrowhead. If we generate the diagram from the preceding definition, it looks like so:

We're now able to add both synchronous and asynchronous messages to our sequence diagrams, which in today's modern world of microservices, is critical. Now that we've added more interactions to our diagram, it can be hard to see where one request begins and ends, and that's where activations come in.

Change Participant Order

Earlier I mentioned there were other reasons to list the participants explicitly. Using the preceding definition, try moving the line defining Kafka as a participant under the Browser definition.

As you can see, defining the participants allows you to change the order they're displayed on the rendered diagram. The default ordering is usually fine, but if you want to highlight a specific service earlier in the diagram, which is only interacted with later on, you can do so.

Display Length of Interactions with Activations

Our sequence diagram is now complete in terms of the interactions we want to document. However, we can add some nice extras to our diagram to make it even more readable.

Firstly, we can clearly show when a request starts and its respective response is received using activations. In essence, a rectangle will be added from the point the request starts to the point the response is returned that shows roughly how many messages that interaction takes.

Naturally, this isn't a reflection on the actual time that part of the process might take to complete when coded, but it does easily show where the more complex parts might be as well as offer improved readability from being able to clearly see the start and end points. How the activations will look on a rendered diagram is shown on page 31.

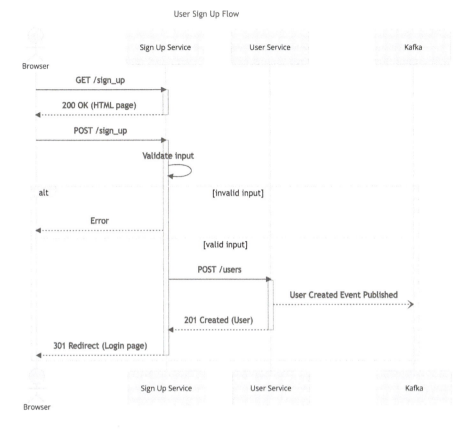

At a glance, we can now see that the main complexity when implementing this flow is likely to be in the POST request from the browser to the sign up service. Here's how to define activations on your sequence diagrams:

```
---
title: User Sign Up Flow
---
sequenceDiagram
    actor Browser
    participant Sign Up Service
    participant User Service
    participant Kafka

    Browser->>Sign Up Service: GET /sign_up
    activate Sign Up Service
    Sign Up Service-->>Browser: 200 OK (HTML page)
    deactivate Sign Up Service

    Browser->>+Sign Up Service: POST /sign_up
    Sign Up Service->>Sign Up Service: Validate input
```

```
    alt invalid input
        Sign Up Service-->>Browser: Error
    else valid input
        Sign Up Service->>+User Service: POST /users
        User Service--)Kafka: User Created Event Published
        User Service-->>-Sign Up Service: 201 Created (User)
        Sign Up Service-->>-Browser: 301 Redirect (Login page)
    end
```

Mermaid has two ways to do this. The first can be seen in the initial GET request, where we have explicit lines for the activations and deactivations. The remaining activations are defined by adding a + (activation) or - (deactivation) sign to the ends of the arrows, like this for example:

```
Sign Up Service->>+User Service: POST /users
User Service--)Kafka: User Created Event Published
User Service-->>-Sign Up Service: 201 Created (User)
```

Both are perfectly valid, and in this case I'll leave it up to you to decide which you prefer. The explicit lines for activations are easier to spot, but the inline activations are more succinct and bloat the definition less.

Whichever you choose, Mermaid allows you to add further clarity to your diagrams by using activations.

That's the last bit of syntax we need for the actual interactions, but we can further enrich our sequence diagram using more of Mermaid's features!

Add Additional Information with Notes

The final element we can add to a sequence diagram is a note, which does exactly what you'd expect. Labels should be kept small, but if you need to add additional context or want to highlight a particular part of the sequence, notes are what you should use.

The final version of our definition, with a note, looks like this:

```
---
title: User Sign Up Flow
---
sequenceDiagram
    actor Browser
    participant Sign Up Service
    participant User Service
    participant Kafka

    Browser->>Sign Up Service: GET /sign_up
    activate Sign Up Service
    Sign Up Service-->>Browser: 200 OK (HTML page)
    deactivate Sign Up Service
```

```
Browser->>+Sign Up Service: POST /sign_up
Sign Up Service->>Sign Up Service: Validate input

alt invalid input
    Sign Up Service-->>Browser: Error
else valid input
    Sign Up Service->>+User Service: POST /users
    User Service--)Kafka: User Created Event Published
    Note left of Kafka: other services take action based on this event
    User Service-->>-Sign Up Service: 201 Created (User)
    Sign Up Service-->>-Browser: 301 Redirect (Login page)
end
```

We've added a note when publishing the message to Kafka, calling out that other downstream services consume this event. The syntax is simple:

```
Note [Left|Right] of [Node]
```

The note displays like so:

I almost always put the notes next to the node they are talking about, but you can put any node name and the note will appear next to that node—you can try this by changing the note line to be Note left of Browser.

You can also span a note across two nodes—for example, if we wanted to span our note across both Kafka and the user service, we could do the following:

```
Note over User Service, Kafka: other services take action based on this event
```

Notes allow you to add more detail to your sequence diagrams; just don't overload the diagram with notes or write especially long notes. They should be used to supplement the main sequence and, for the most part, shouldn't be necessary to understand the core flow. For example, I recently used a note when showing an HTTP call to an external API to highlight that we needed to pass a JSON web token (JWT) in the request as a form of authentication. That was a necessary detail that I wanted to draw attention to.

Mermaid provides one more feature that I've always found incredibly useful, and that's annotating the diagram with sequence numbers. We'll take a look at that in the next section.

Annotate Your Diagram with Sequence Numbers

In terms of the interactions on our sequence diagram, I think we're done! But before we move on, there's a little more Mermaid magic I want to show you to really make your diagram pop.

Firstly, Mermaid can provide automatic sequence numbering. This essentially adds a number to each message on the diagram, which is particularly useful when discussing the diagram with colleagues. It can be a bit confusing to try to describe which particular part of the diagram you're making a point about, but with numbers that becomes a breeze.

We can add sequence numbers to our diagram by adding autonumber below the sequenceDiagram line. If we added sequence numbers to our diagram, the first section would look like this:

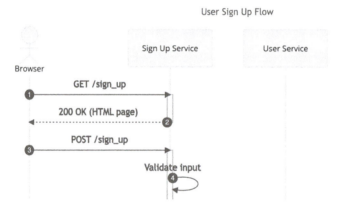

As you can see, pointing to specific sections would now be easy, as would showing the total number of interactions by looking at the last interaction.

Create Dropdown Menus

A useful feature for sequence diagrams in Mermaid is the ability to add menus to each actor or participant. This allows you to enrich the diagram with useful links—for example, linking to a service's repository, its domain model, or documentation for why the service was created (such as an architecture decision record).

Adding links is done using a JSON-like format, like so:

```
links User Service: {"Repository": "https://www.example.com/repository"}
```

You may add as many key-value pairs as you like to the drop-down.

When rendered, and the mouse is hovered over the actor or participant, this is how the menu will look:

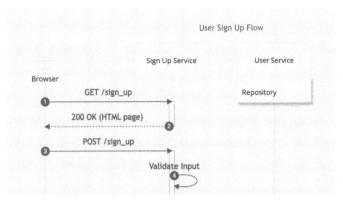

Keep in mind, the drop-down menus will only work on rendered pages; they won't be visible on static images or printed pages.

Visualize Your Own Application Flow

Now it's your chance to create a sequence diagram for one of the flows for the project you picked in Document Your Own Domain, on page 8. Try to pick one that has some complicated elements to it to make use of all the things you've learned in this chapter.

You don't have to use the same company for each diagram, but it might help to keep the same one, if possible, to save context switching between different domains and projects.

As a bonus activity, next time you come across some code that's a little complex and hard to grasp initially, try writing a sequence diagram for the interactions to see if that helps uncover how it all fits together.

What You've Learned

Before you have a go at creating your own sequence diagram, let's review what you learned in this chapter:

1. What a sequence diagram is, and what it can be used for.

2. How to define the actors and participants in play in the sequence diagram.

3. How to add interactions between actors and participants.

4. How to show branching logic and asynchronous messages.

5. How you can improve readability with activations to show the length of an interaction.

6. How you can enrich diagrams with sequence numbers and additional context using notes.

7. That, besides system interactions, sequence diagrams can be used to understand interactions between classes.

A sequence diagram is used to understand the interactions between different actors and participants in any given flow. You define actors and participants using actor and participant, respectively, and then define interactions between them using arrow-like syntax such as -->>. Sequence diagrams regularly have branches, which can be added using the alt, else, and end syntax. You can improve the readability of your diagrams by using + and - activations and help others talk about specific interactions with sequence numbers. Finally, you can add notes to call out small but essential details using Note left of X: your note here.

To bring everything together, the final result from this chapter looks like this:

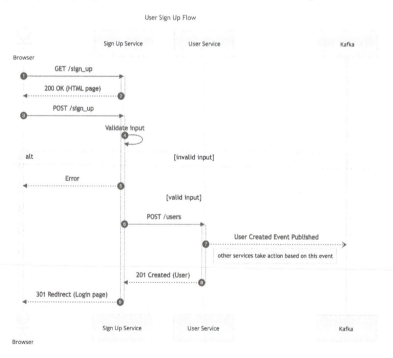

Now that we have visualized the flows for an application, we can move on to the next step in building out our software system: designing and documenting the architecture for a given system.

## CHAPTER 4

Model Your Architecture

Similarly to writing code, we want to do just enough design up front to validate our approach but not so much there's no room for the design to evolve over time. If your role includes designing architectural solutions, you should aim to document the architecture enough so that it's a solid guide for teams implementing the design but still leaves plenty of room for them to be creative and sculpt the final product.

This book is not a book on how to be a software architect, but it's important to understand how diagrams should be used. They shouldn't be created in isolation and handed down to engineers to interpret and implement. If you're responsible for designing a software system, ensure you embed yourself closely with the team building that software system. Seek regular feedback from that team, as well as peers such as other architects, and ideally collaboratively evolve the design with your colleagues.

This is a huge selling point for using Mermaid, as it allows us to quickly iterate over any diagram simply by changing some simple definitions. In days of old, before I started using Mermaid, a part of me would be disheartened when I had to change a diagram I'd made using a UI-based tool—not because I wasn't open to change, but because changing that diagram was painstakingly painful. Having to move all the boxes, redraw lines, and so on, could take several hours if the change was significant.

Once you're used to Mermaid's syntax, you can live-edit your architecture diagrams (and other diagrams) while in a meeting with a colleague. You can try out an idea in minutes, and if it's not an improvement, throw it away with no significant time wasted.

In this chapter, and the following two chapters, you'll learn how to create diagrams to represent your architecture. Once again, we'll leverage Mermaid to create the diagrams, but this time we won't be using UML. Mermaid supports an array of diagram types that sit outside of UML, and in this chapter you'll learn how we can use flowcharts to implement the C4 model for visualizing your software architecture.

One of the best use cases for the C4 model is in your project's README. Whenever someone wants to know about your project, they probably go to the README first. In each of the projects that my team owns, you'll find a C4 model. Recently, the company went through a restructure, and some projects got reassigned to different teams. This required hand over to another team, and the C4 model was the perfect piece of documentation to easily explain to another team how the system worked. The same can be said for new joiners—they can quickly and easily see exactly how a service operates by looking at the C4 model in the README.

The C4 model is also useful when creating ADRs, similarly to the prior chapter. When creating an ADR, you're essentially proposing the design of the system, so you can use the C4 model to quickly iterate through ideas for your architecture.

Now that we've discussed some of the use cases for the C4 model, let's take a look at it in detail.

Using the C4 Model

Before we get into creating diagrams, though, let's step back and examine what the C4 model is, why it was created, and how it helps us.

The C4 model consists of four parts, with each part containing a different view of our architecture and gradually increasing in detail as we move through the four parts.

> The C4 model was inspired by the Unified Modeling Language and the 4+1 model for software architecture. In summary, you can think of the C4 model as a simplified version of the underlying concepts, designed to (1) make it easier for software developers to describe and understand how a software system works and (2) to minimize the gap between the software architecture model/description and the source code.[1]

The C4 model was created by Simon Brown as a consistent mechanism for teams to model their software architecture, and the preceding description is his.

As mentioned, a C4 diagram has four parts:

---

1. https://c4model.com/

- System context
- Container
- Component
- Code

As we move through each part, we zoom in a little further in terms of detail, and the details provided get more and more technical. If the system context diagram is the 50,000-foot view, the code diagram is the microscopic view. We'll only be creating the first three and leaving out the code diagram for now.

Lastly, there's no defined notation for creating C4 diagrams. There's no guide that says to use solid lines for X and dashed lines for Y or use black to denote A and blue to denote B. C4 just lays out the framework for the details captured at each level of the C4 model, but we'll be sticking closely to the notation used by Simon Brown. If you want to tweak it as you build your own diagrams, go ahead—just remember to keep your notation consistent across the different parts.

Creating a System Context Diagram

Let's start with the highest-level view, the system context diagram. It is the 50,000-foot view, so contains the minimal level of detail of our architecture. It should be nontechnical and simply acts to model the interactions between users of the system you're designing and any other systems in play.

The litmus test you can use to determine if the level of detail is correct is whether I could show it to my product manager, or anyone nontechnical, and they would be able to understand what the diagram is trying to convey. If they can, you know it's the right level. It's not useful just for product managers though; it's key in understanding at a glance what your system's key dependencies are and how it undertakes its responsibilities.

Continuing on the journey of Streamy, we're going to design an architecture for the service that is responsible for displaying the lists of titles available to view on the platform. In essence, when a user goes to the platform, what does the listings service need to do to show the titles, and how does it do it?

A second requirement is that when a title is displayed, the reviews for that title are also displayed, and the user has the option to submit a review for that title if they wish.

Thirdly, listings are great, but the user should also be able to search for specific titles if they want to watch a particular one.

Finally, other engineering teams at Streamy have been busy creating services to support the upcoming launch. Three services are already available for us to use: a title service, a review service, and a search service.

In a real-world scenario, this kind of information would be either readily known by you or your team or it would be discovered as part of this exercise.

As mentioned in Using the C4 Model, on page 38, there are three main elements in a system context diagram:

- People
- Your software system (that you are designing)
- Supporting software systems

Let's work from top to bottom and start forming our system context diagram. We'll be using a flowchart, supported by Mermaid. Flowcharts are extremely versatile and, unlike the prior diagrams we covered, don't have a single use case. We're going to use them to create C4 diagrams, but you could also use them to diagram a business use case, as they support branched logic quite well. If you need to create something that doesn't fit in any of the use cases covered in this book, you can likely create it using a flowchart.

We now understand what we're trying to accomplish and how we plan to do it, so let's get started!

Add Nodes

Let's get started by defining a flowchart and our first element, the user:

```
flowchart TD
    User["Premium Member
    [Person]

    A user of the website who has
    purchased a subscription"]
```

Nodes also support adding in new lines (\n) in text, which I prefer to use rather than actual new lines in the diagram's code, as I find it harder to read. The lines aren't actually that long, but for a book, they need to be smaller, so I've used this format.

Once generated, it looks like the image shown on page 41.

In this example only one person is being shown, but it's not uncommon to have multiple users interacting with your system in different ways, so make sure to include everyone.

```
Premium Member
[Person]

A user of the website who has
purchased a subscription
```

As with all Mermaid diagrams, the first line defines the type of diagram we're creating—in our case, flowchart. There's an optional parameter you can define after flowchart that defines the direction, which accepts the following options:

- *TB*: top-to-bottom
- *TD*: top-down (same as top-to-bottom)
- *BT*: bottom-to-top
- *RL*: right-to-left
- *LR*: left-to-right

We'll be using top-down as that suits our use case.

The second line defines a *node* in our flowchart. You can think of this like defining a class before you use it in your codebase: the node is only defined once and then used where it's needed later on. This allows you to define certain characteristics for a node once, and it will be used automatically throughout the flow.

All node definitions follow the format id["Label / Description"]. The ID is the reference you'll use when defining the interactions later on, so I tend to keep them short, and the label/description is the text that goes in the box that's rendered.

Following Simon Brown's notation, each node should contain a title, label, and description. The title should clearly outline the node, the label is what type the node is, and the description briefly describes what that node represents. At this level, the label is perhaps superfluous, but in more detailed views that follow, it's essential, and I like to keep the layout consistent between the different levels of the C4 model.

We can't make much of a diagram with just a single node, so next we add our system—the system we're designing and documenting with the C4 model. The Mermaid definition now looks like this:

```
flowchart TD
  User["Premium Member
  [Person]
```

```
A user of the website who has
purchased a subscription"]

LS["Listings Service
[Software System]

Serves web pages displaying title
listings to the end user"]
```

As nothing is connected yet, we now have two isolated nodes displayed:

 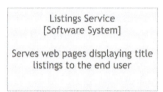

Nodes on their own don't provide much value though, so let's try connecting these nodes.

Connect Nodes

Now the fun begins! We can connect our two nodes in a flowchart using a variety of arrows, but for a system context diagram we just need simple solid arrowheads that show dependencies. We can add an interaction between nodes like so:

```
flowchart TD
    User["Premium Member
    [Person]

    A user of the website who has\npurchased a subscription"]

    LS["Listings Service
    [Software System]

    Serves web pages displaying title
    listings to the end user"]

    User-- "Views titles, searches titles\nand reviews titles using" -->LS
```

You can define arrows in two different styles, so pick your preference. We can use the one shown previously that follows the format ParentNode-- "arrow label" -->ChildNode, or we can use the format ParentNode-->|"arrow label"|ChildNode. I personally find the former easier to read, but both work in exactly the same way. The double quotes are optional but are required later on for more detailed labels, so you'll want to get into the habit of using them now.

If we generate this diagram, we can now see the two nodes linked, as shown on page 43.

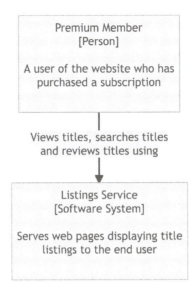

I've modeled the arrows as dependencies, so for the arrow label I simply describe what the parent node relies on from the child node. You don't need to go into large amounts of detail, especially at this level, so try to keep the descriptions brief.

We now have the people interacting with our system. And our new system, on the system context diagram, just one more thing is left to add: supporting systems. These are any systems that your system interacts with and that are required for it to do its job. They can be other internal systems or external systems provided by another company, such as Salesforce if you use that for your customer relationship management (CRM).

In our case, we determined earlier (Creating a System Context Diagram, on page 39) that there were three supporting systems already available to use at Streamy: the title service, the review service, and the search service, so let's add them to our system context diagram.

```
flowchart TD
    User["Premium Member
    [Person]

    A user of the website who has
    purchased a subscription"]

    LS["Listings Service
    [Software System]

    Serves web pages displaying title
    listings to the end user"]
```

```
TS["Title Service
[Software System]

Provides an API to retrieve
title information"]

RS["Review Service
[Software System]

Provides an API to retrieve
and submit reviews"]

SS["Search Service
[Software System]

Provides an API to search
for titles"]

User-- "Views titles, searches titles\nand reviews titles using" -->LS

LS-- "Retrieves title information from" -->TS
LS-- "Retrieves from and submits reviews to" -->RS
LS-- "Searches for titles using" -->SS
```

Once generated, we have a completed system context diagram!

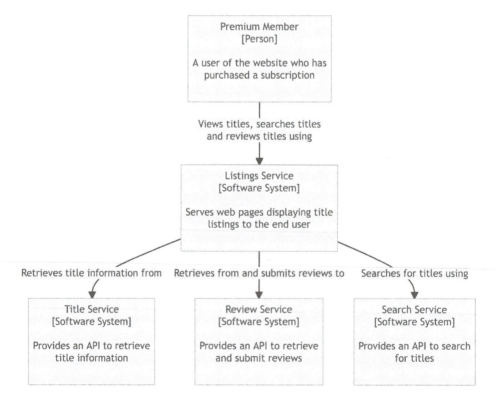

Using this diagram, both technical and nontechnical colleagues can understand at a high level who uses your system, what your system does, and how it does it in combination with other systems. That documentation alone is *probably* more detailed than most repository READMEs and will answer several initial questions anyone has when they want to know about your new system.

Adding HTTP Links to Nodes

Do you remember that for class diagrams you can add links to nodes? You can do exactly the same for flowcharts, using exactly the same syntax!

Add Some Style

We can, however, leverage one last feature from Mermaid to make the diagram a bit easier on the eyes. I'm not a fan of adding style for style's sake, but when looking at the C4 model, I think color is really powerful for clearly highlighting what each node represents.

Borrowing from Simon Brown's notation once again, let's employ a simple color palette for that. The system context diagram has dark blue for people, a lighter blue for your system, and gray for supporting systems. Styling is simple to do, using a combination of CSS and SVG styling options. I found CSS Tricks[2] has an excellent guide for understanding what properties to use.

We can add styling to our nodes using the following:

```
---
title: "Listing Service C4 Model: System Context"
---
flowchart TD
    User["Premium Member
    [Person]

    A user of the website who has
    purchased a subscription"]

    LS["Listings Service
    [Software System]

    Serves web pages displaying title
    listings to the end user"]

    TS["Title Service
    [Software System]
```

---

2. https://css-tricks.com/svg-properties-and-css/Borrowing

```
    Provides an API to retrieve
    title information"]

    RS["Review Service
    [Software System]

    Provides an API to retrieve
    and submit reviews"]

    SS["Search Service
    [Software System]

    Provides an API to search
    for titles"]

    User-- "Views titles, searches titles\nand reviews titles using" -->LS

    LS-- "Retrieves title information from" -->TS
    LS-- "Retrieves from and submits reviews to" -->RS
    LS-- "Searches for titles using" -->SS

    classDef focusSystem fill:#1168bd,stroke:#0b4884,color:#ffffff
    classDef supportingSystem fill:#666,stroke:#0b4884,color:#ffffff
    classDef person fill:#08427b,stroke:#052e56,color:#ffffff

    class User person
    class LS focusSystem
    class TS,RS,SS supportingSystem
```

I also added a title to the diagram at this point. Notice how I wrapped the title text in double quotes this time, as the title text contains a colon. Once generated, we now have colors and a title on our diagram, as shown on page 47.

There are two parts to adding styling to our nodes. First, we define a class using the syntax classDef className styleProperties. Once the class is defined, we can then use that style on any nodes simply by attaching that class using the syntax class nodeId(s) className.

You can also attach the same class to multiple nodes in one line, which you can see on the last line of the diagram definition.

Generally, choose to put all of the styling at the end of the diagram to keep the actual diagram definition and interactions as clean and readable as possible. Keep in mind, color shouldn't be necessary to read a diagram but should be used to supplement a diagram.

Having said that, if you're reading this without color, I highly recommend viewing the generated diagram at this point to really see how color can enhance the clarity of a diagram.

As it's a high-level diagram, that's it for the system context diagram—so time for you to try creating your own.

Listing Service C4 Model: System Context

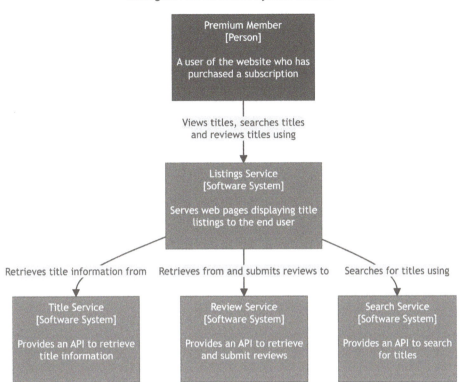

Create Your Own System Context Diagram

Now it's your turn once again! In the next chapter we'll cover the container diagram, a much more detailed view of our architecture, but before that go ahead and create a system context diagram for the project you're using for the exercises in this book.

Simply pick a system you know you would need to build for your project, or pick a system you've previously worked on, and draw the system context diagram for that system.

What You've Learned

You've learned that a system context diagram should be a nontechnical diagram that outlines the highest-level view of your architecture: the systems. It should be readable by anyone in the business, including nontechnical colleagues.

With that in mind, you then learned what information to put on a system context diagram: the actors and systems in your architecture, with a brief description for each, and linking them all together and describing the interactions between them.

It's important to establish this high-level view of your systems so that anyone can understand it at a glance. But this doesn't go into enough detail for most engineers to really understand how a system works. In the next chapter, we'll zoom in a little further into our architecture and document the individual units that make up our system.

## CHAPTER 5

Detail Your System's Containers

We've just covered how to document the systems in play in the scope of a single system. That provides a great high-level overview to anyone looking at the diagram and will answer the questions that most nontechnical colleagues have. However, most engineers will want more detail than the system context diagram provides. They want to get into the technical details; they want to understand the different parts that make up your system and the means with which it communicates with other systems.

That's where the container diagram comes in. It starts to get into the technical details of your system's architecture. Not to be confused with Docker containers, in C4 a container simply means a single deployable unit. For example, in a very simple system, you might have a Java application as one container and a Postgres database as a second container, and that's it.

Container diagrams still don't get into the nitty-gritty—they show no details about the actual code of any of the containers. The format is similar to the system context diagram, in that it still shows interactions, but this time the focus is on interactions between containers rather than systems.

Going back to the zoom analogy, container diagrams zoom in on the system you're modeling to show everything deployed for that system to function. You can think of it like clicking the Listing Service node from the system context diagram and it then zooming into that system.

For our example of displaying title listings to the user, three containers are in play:

- A mobile application for mobile users

- A web application that serves web browsers and also hosts an API for the mobile app to retrieve/send data to/from

- A Redis instance for caching, to prevent repeated API calls to downstream services, such as the title service

Finally, we also have a message broker in the form of Kafka, that we send domain events to when important things happen (for example, a user views listings or a user watches a title). Due to the nature of a message broker, that sits at the enterprise level and is used by multiple systems, so it's a supporting service. I opted not to include this on the system context diagram as it's largely a technical consideration, and technical details shouldn't be included at the system context level.

While the system context diagram is excellent for engineers and non-engineers alike, the container diagram is going to really help engineers at Streamy understand the target architecture. So we can provide that information to them, let's get started with the container diagram.

Define the First Two Containers

Once again, we're going to use a flowchart. The container diagram still includes the people interacting with the system at the top, so let's add the two containers our user interacts with first—the web application and the mobile application:

```
flowchart TD
    User["Premium Member
    [Person]
    A user of the website who has
    purchased a subscription"]

    WA["Web Application
    [.NET Core MVC Application]
    Allows members to view and review titles
    from a web browser. Also exposes
    an API for the mobile app"]

    MA["Mobile Application
    [Xamarin Application]
    Allows members to view and review
    titles from their mobile devices"]

    User-- "Views titles, searches titles
    and reviews titles using
    [HTTPS]" -->WA

    User-- "Views titles, searches titles
    and reviews titles using
    [HTTPS]" -->MA
```

```
classDef container fill:#1168bd,stroke:#0b4884,color:#ffffff
classDef person fill:#08427b,stroke:#052e56,color:#ffffff
class User person
class WA,MA container
```

This should look familiar, as it's exactly the same syntax as we used in the system context diagram. However, we're now adding in more detail. Firstly, we've added the technologies used within each container; for example, the web application is a .NET Core MVC Application. Secondly, we've added the protocol when two nodes communicate with each other—for now both interactions are via HTTPS.

We're sticking with the same styling as before, and as we're zoomed in on our system, the containers are the same color as the focus system in the system context diagram.

Once generated, we have the start of our container diagram:

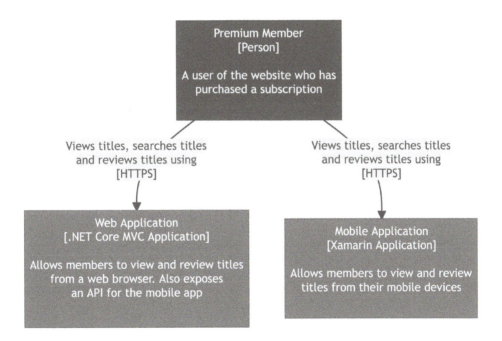

We have quite a few more elements to add to our container diagram, but first let's look at how we can differentiate the nodes within our system from those outside our system.

Create Clear Boundaries with Subgraphs

To handle the expected demand at Streamy, they want to leverage a Redis cache to prevent repeated calls to downstream APIs.

We now want to add that final Redis container and add the interaction between the mobile application and the web application.

I find it useful to display the boundary of the system on the container diagram, in case the colors aren't clear enough. For that, we can leverage what's called a subgraph in a flowchart. Anything within that boundary belongs to the system we're architecting. I think of it like the lens for this diagram, where we've zoomed in one one of the boxes from the system context diagram. We can add the boundary, using a subgraph, like so:

```
flowchart TD
    User["Premium Member
    [Person]

    A user of the website who has
    purchased a subscription"]

    WA["Web Application
    [.NET Core MVC Application]

    Allows members to view and review titles
    from a web browser. Also exposes
    an API for the mobile app"]

    MA["Mobile Application
    [Xamarin Application]

    Allows members to view and review
    titles from their mobile devices"]

    R[("In-Memory Cache
    [Redis]

    Titles and their reviews
    are cached")]

    User-- "Views titles, searches titles
    and reviews titles using
    [HTTPS]" -->WA

    User-- "Views titles, searches titles
    and reviews titles using
    [HTTPS]" -->MA

    subgraph listing-service[Listing Service]
        MA-- "Makes API calls to\n[HTTPS]" -->WA

        WA-- "Reads and writes to\n[REdis Serialization Protocol]" -->R
    end
```

```
classDef container fill:#1168bd,stroke:#0b4884,color:#ffffff
classDef person fill:#08427b,stroke:#052e56,color:#ffffff
class User person
class WA,MA,R container
style listing-service fill:none,stroke:#CCC,stroke-width:2px
style listing-service color:#fff,stroke-dasharray: 5 5
```

The style line can, and should, be a single line with all the styling properties on one line. It's just on separate lines for readability within the book and still renders the same.

Most of the syntax should now look familiar to you, certainly in terms of the addition of Redis as a node below the mobile application and the way in which we draw interactions between containers.

However, I'd like to draw your attention to three new pieces of functionality:

1. We've added a subgraph, which takes a single parameter id[Title] that allows us to define subflows within the main flowchart. In a programming or logic sense, these would be akin to subroutines, but for C4 diagrams, they're an excellent way to differentiate your system's containers, within a boundary, from the rest of the nodes.

2. Now that we have a boundary defined, using a subgraph, I've styled it using a style line on the last line. This is an alternative way to define styles versus using a classDef,and I use style lines if there's just one node needing a single style. It follows the format style nodeId styleProperties. By default, the boundary would be a somewhat vibrant yellow, so I've changed it to be a simple dashed border.

3. When we defined the Redis node, we added circular brackets around the label text. This changes the node shape from a rectangle to a cylinder, which is regularly used in a diagram to represent a datastore of some kind.

To ensure the boundary is accurate, make sure you *only* put interactions in the subgraph that contains interactions where both nodes are part of the system you're modeling.

Once generated, the container diagram looks like the diagram shown on page 54.

We can also add more technical descriptions where applicable, whereas the web and mobile applications are pretty low-tech. We can talk about caching when we add the Redis instance.

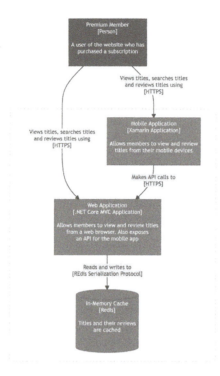

We've now successfully added the containers that our system consists of, but what about supporting systems that it utilizes?

Additional Flowchart Shapes

A variety of shapes besides rectangles and cylinders are available to use within flowcharts. The main other two I use are circles, which are formed using id((label)), and diamonds, formed using id{label}. A full list is available from Mermaid's documentation.[1]

Add Supporting Systems

In the previous chapter Creating a System Context Diagram, on page 39, we also identified several supporting systems that our system needs to function. To finish adding nodes to our container diagram, we now need to add supporting systems and show the interactions between our system's containers and the suppporting systems. Let's do so now:

```
flowchart TD
    User["Premium Member
    [Person]
```

---

1.   https://mermaid-js.github.io/mermaid/#/flowchart?id=node-shapes

```
A user of the website who has
purchased a subscription"]

WA["Web Application
[.NET Core MVC Application]

Allows members to view and review titles
from a web browser. Also exposes
an API for the mobile app"]

MA["Mobile Application
[Xamarin Application]

Allows members to view and review
titles from their mobile devices"]

R[("In-Memory Cache
[Redis]

Titles and their reviews
are cached")]

K["Message Broker
[Kafka]

Important domain events
are published to Kafka"]

TS["Title Service
[Software System]

Provides an API to retrieve
title information"]

RS["Reviews Service
[Software System]

Provides an API to retrieve
and submit reviews"]

SS["Search Service
[Software System]

Provides an API to search
for titles"]

User-- "Views titles, searches titles
and reviews titles using
[HTTPS]" -->WA

User-- "Views titles, searches titles
and reviews titles using
[HTTPS]" -->MA

subgraph listing-service[Listing Service]
    MA-- "Makes API calls to\n[HTTPS]" -->WA

    WA-- "Reads and writes to\n[REdis Serialization Protocol]" -->R
end
```

```
WA-- "Publishes messages to\n[Binary over TCP]" -->K
WA-- "Makes API calls to\n[HTTPS]" -->TS
WA-- "Makes API calls to\n[HTTPS]" -->RS
WA-- "Makes API calls to\n[HTTPS]" -->SS

classDef container fill:#1168bd,stroke:#0b4884,color:#ffffff
classDef person fill:#08427b,stroke:#052e56,color:#ffffff
classDef supportingSystem fill:#666,stroke:#0b4884,color:#ffffff
class User person
class WA,MA,R container
class TS,RS,SS,K supportingSystem
style listing-service fill:none,stroke:#CCC,stroke-width:2px
style listing-service color:#fff,stroke-dasharray: 5 5
```

All of this syntax is familar to you now; we simply added the supporting nodes at the top and added the interactions between them and our system's containers below the subgraph. Let's see what the container diagram looks like now:

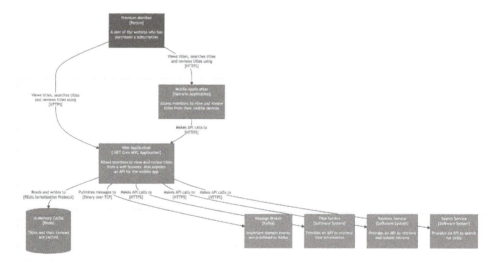

Well, all the information is certainly there, but it looks a little funny with the arrows flying off to the right. It also makes the diagram very wide, making it much harder to read. Wouldn't it be nice if the gray boxes sat below the boundary of our system?

Improve Readability with Link Lengths

Luckily, we can force Mermaid to do that. To understand how, flowcharts work off of ranks. For example, the person is rank 1 and the mobile application is rank 2. Mermaid will automatically rank nodes based on the definition, which you can see at play with the web application. Because there's an interaction between the mobile application and the web application, a child node will always sit below its parent, so the web application sits at rank 3.

To show this visually, we can update the subgraph in our current container diagram to remove the interaction between the mobile application and web application, like so:

```
subgraph listing-service[Listing Service]
    WA-- "Reads and writes to\n[REdis Serialization Protocol]" -->R

    MA
end
```

The web and mobile application nodes now sit side by side on rank 2:

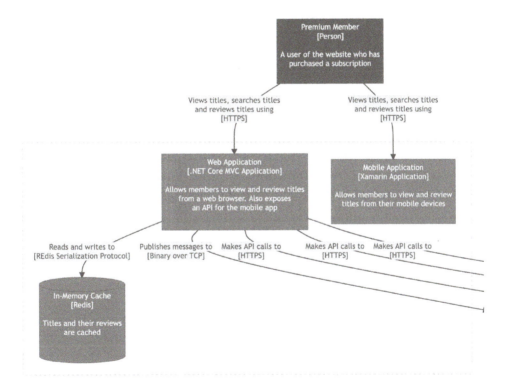

Note that we still define the mobile application, with no interactions defined, simply to force Mermaid to put the mobile application within our boundary.

You might be wondering how this ties into our original problem: how do we force the gray boxes to display a little nicer?

Well, currently Mermaid is putting the gray boxes at the same rank as Redis, which is causing this somewhat strange-looking diagram. However, we can *request* Mermaid increase the rank of any interaction by increasing the number of elements in our arrows. The key word here is *request*, as Mermaid might not be able to fulfil it in all cases, depending on the interactions, as it may break the diagram.

Please note: if you made the preceding code change to remove the interaction between the mobile and web application, please replace it now before making the code adjustments, as we only made that change to visually understand how ranks work in Mermaid's rendering.

Here's the updated interaction definitions for our supporting services:

```
WA-- "Publishes messages to\n[Binary over TCP]" --->K
WA-- "Makes API calls to\n[HTTPS]" --->TS
WA-- "Makes API calls to\n[HTTPS]" --->RS
WA-- "Makes API calls to\n[HTTPS]" --->SS
```

All that changed was an extra hyphen before the child nodes, and now the diagram renders as shown on page 59.

I think we can agree, this looks much better. As you get used to Mermaid, you'll find making changes like this becomes natural to optimize the Mermaid rendering. Luckily, due to the ability to rapidly iterate over diagrams with Mermaid, restructuring a diagram is quick and simple, and you can play around with the ranks until you get it how you want.

Another occasion I adjust the ranks is if the lines or descriptions feel a little bunched. We can artificially create more space between nodes by adding longer lines, as we just did here. If we add hyphens to all interactions at a given rank, Mermaid essentially "skips" a rank and simply fills the rank with an extended line.

You'll notice I added the title too, using the same syntax we learned in the previous chapters. You can add the title to your diagrams at any point. For me it's like signing off a diagram when I give it a title—I then deem it complete.

So far, we've only covered synchronous interactions between containers. Can we use different syntax to easily show asynchronous communication?

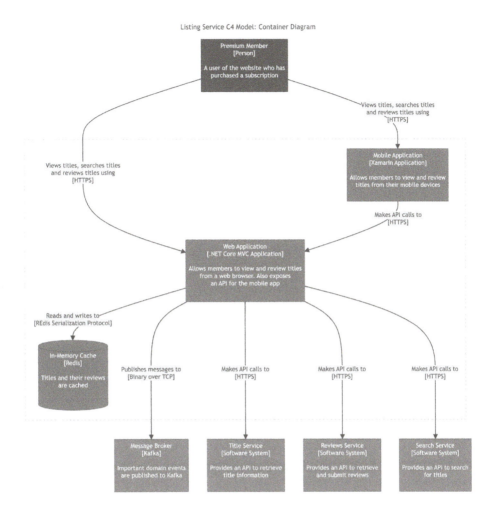

Display Asynchronous Interactions

Finally, you may wish to differentiate synchronous and asynchronous communication clearly in your container diagrams—I personally do. Our example exclusively has synchronous communication, so all of the arrows are solid.

However, the interaction between the web application and the message broker is asynchronous, so we can change the solid line to a dotted line by adjusting the interaction definition to the following:

```
WA-. "Publishes messages to\n[Binary over TCP]" ..->K
```

This causes the line to now display as dotted:

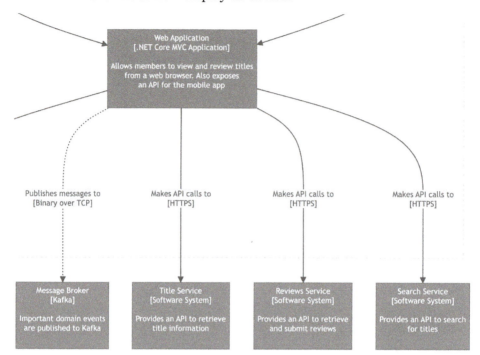

The base syntax for a dashed line is ParentNode-. "arrow text" .->ChildNode, but we used two dots, as we want to make use of extending the rank of that interaction, which is done with extra dots, rather than hyphens, for dotted lines.

You can use a few more arrow types in flowcharts—let's take a look at them before we wrap up this chapter.

Additional Arrow Types

I've highlighted the arrows I most commonly use, but for completeness, there is a list shown on page 61 of all the supported arrow types in Mermaid flowcharts. I've also included some alternative syntax for some arrows we've used already, in case you prefer the alternative.

That completes the container diagram, and by now you know the drill—it's your turn to create a diagram.

Create Your Own Container Diagram

That wraps it up for the container diagram! In the next chapter we'll cover the component diagram, but first have a go at creating the container diagram, using the format and techniques you learned in this chapter.

Example	Description	Syntax
	Link with Arrowhead	A->B
	Link with Arrowhead (with text)	A- text ->B or A->|text|B
	Link with No Arrowhead	A—B
	Link with No Arrowhead (with text)	A- This is the text! —B or A— |This is the text|B
	Dotted Link	A-.->B
	Dotted Link (with text)	A-. text .-> B
	Thick Link with Arrowhead	A ==> B
	Thick Link with Arrowhead (with text)	A == text ==> B
	Chaining Links	A- text -> B - text2 -> C
	Multiple Links	A -> B & C-> D

You can use your system context diagram from Creating a System Context Diagram, on page 39, as the base and build out the containers within the focus system.

What You've Learned

That's all for container diagrams, so let's review what we've covered in this chapter.

You learned that a container diagram details each deployable unit in your architecture and drills into the details of the focus system for this set of C4 diagrams. Each node should represent something that is deployed within your architecture and provide a little detail about that deployable unit, such as the languages or frameworks, and a brief description on its role. Finally, we link all the nodes together to document how they communicate to execute their purpose in our architecture.

## CHAPTER 6

Structure Your Components and Code

We've now created a system context diagram and a container diagram. When combined, they show a high-level overview of our system, its users, its supporting systems, and the individual deployable units that make up our system. For most use cases, that will be enough detail, but in case you want to delve a little deeper, we're going to briefly cover the component diagram in C4.

The component diagram once again zooms in further in terms of technical detail and highlights the major components within *each* container.

Component can mean many different things and has become overloaded in the tech industry, but within C4 it's the equivalent of a high-level namespace or module, or some sort of library or package that's included in the container.

We don't need to go into depths of detail and include every namespace or library, but just deep enough to highlight the major building blocks of each container. It's worth noting that the guidance from the C4 model website lists this diagram as optional, as the diagram can become quickly out-of-date as code is worked on.

I think there's value in adding component diagrams for larger systems—for example, a modular monolith, where the high-level components often map to domains. Furthermore, if you have a modular monolith, a single container doesn't really do justice to the architecture you've opted for, so the component diagram fills in the blanks.

Conversely, if you're working with more granular microservices, the component diagrams are likely wasted effort, as the majority of the useful information can be understood from the container diagram, with the microservice itself containing minimum meaningful components.

Therefore, it's up to you on a case-by-case basis whether there's value in adding the component diagram. For the vast majority of use cases, I would say the system context and container diagram is plenty of detail in terms of documentation and (just enough) up-front design.

No new concepts or features are needed to create a component diagram—we can use what we covered when creating the system context and container diagrams. Therefore, here's a component diagram as an example for the web application container:

```
---
title: "Listing Service C4 Model: Component Diagram"
---
flowchart TD
    classDef container fill:#1168bd,stroke:#0b4884,color:#ffffff
    classDef externalSystem fill:#666,stroke:#0b4884,color:#ffffff
    classDef component fill:#85bbf0,stroke:#5d82a8,color:#000000

    Browser["Browser
    [Web Browser]

    Used by a user to browse
    the website"]

    MA["Application
    [Xamarin Application]

    Allows members to view and review
    titles from their mobile devices"]

    R["In-Memory Cache
    [Redis]

    Titles and their reviews
    are cached"]

    K["Message Broker
    [Kafka]

    Important domain events
    are published to Kafka"]

    TS["Title Service
    [Software System]

    Provides an API to retrieve
    title information"]

    RS["Review Service
    [Software System]

    Provides an API to retrieve
    and submit reviews"]

    SS["Search Service
    [Software System]

    Provides an API to search
    for titles"]
```

```
TCont["Title Controller
[ASP.NET MVC Controller]

Allows users to view details
about titles"]

SCont["Search Controller
[ASP.NET MVC Controller]

Allows users to search
for titles"]

RCont["Review Controller
[ASP.NET MVC Controller]

Allows users to read and
write reviews"]

TComp["Title Component
[ASP.NET Namespace]

Provides information on titles,
retrieves information from the title service
and caches titles"]

SComp["Search Component
[ASP.NET Namespace]

Searches titles using the
search service"]

RComp["Review Component
[ASP.NET Namespace]

Provides review information,
submits new reviews
and publishes domain events"]

Browser-- "Submits requests to\n[HTTPS]" --->TCont
MA-- "Submits requests to\n[HTTPS]" --->TCont

MA-- "Submits requests to\n[HTTPS]" --->SCont
Browser-- "Submits requests to\n[HTTPS]" --->SCont

MA-- "Submits requests to\n[HTTPS]" --->RCont
Browser-- "Submits requests to\n[HTTPS]" --->RCont

subgraph listing-service[Listing Service]
    TCont--->TComp
    RCont--->TComp
    RCont--->RComp

    SCont--->SComp
end

TComp--->TS
TComp--->R
```

```
RComp--->R
RComp--->K
RComp--->RS

SComp--->SS

class MA,R container
class SS,RS,TS,K,Browser externalSystem
class RComp,SComp,TComp,RCont,SCont,TCont component
style listing-service fill:none,stroke:#CCC,stroke-width:2px
style listing-service color:#fff,stroke-dasharray: 5 5
```

The diagram itself is too large to render in full, but part of what the component diagram looks like once generated is shown on page 67.

Once again, we've used a subgraph to define a boundary—this time, the boundary is the web application container. Components within that container are defined with a new style, a pale blue, to differentiate them from components.

We still include the interactions between components and any outside external systems or containers. I find it useful to always include the callers of the components above the boundary—in our case, the mobile application and the web browser. Below the boundary, we still have the external services that are called by components, as well as one of our own containers, the Redis cache.

Keep in mind, each container can have a component diagram, so if you have a lot of containers and decide to create component diagrams, you'll end up creating a large number of component diagrams that you'll need to try to keep up-to-date. Naturally, there's no need to do component diagrams for third-party products such as Redis, as that's essentially a black box that you don't need to model.

That's it for component diagrams. Before finishing the modeling architecture chapters, we'll quickly look at the code diagram in C4, just to understand why creating this level of detail isn't usually worthwhile.

Code Diagram

The final diagram in the set of C4 diagrams is the code diagram. This view of your architecture zooms in once more, this time into each component within each container, and details the classes present within each component.

We're not going to be creating any code diagrams, simply because I've never needed to and would never recommend creating one, at least not manually. The reasons for that are similar to the component diagram but on a much

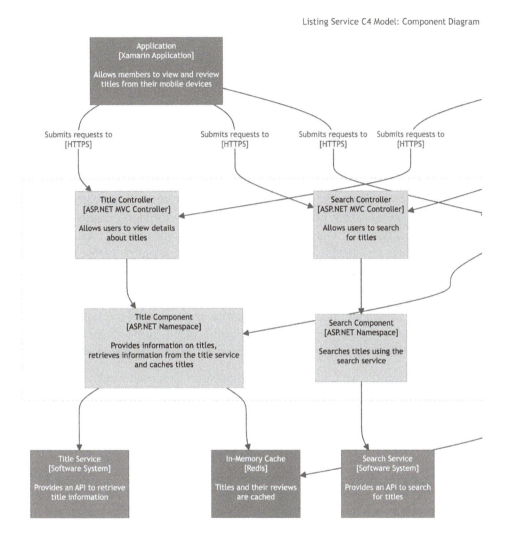

Listing Service C4 Model: Component Diagram

more extreme scale. Code changes so frequently that, if created manually, the code diagram would likely be out of date within days or hours of it being written.

Furthermore, you'd spend just as long keeping the diagrams up-to-date as you would maintaining code, and that's not a good use of anyone's time when they can clearly see the level of detail they need in the code itself. In reality, the diagrams would get created once and rapidly become out-of-date, and there's not much worse in diagramming terms than an out-of-date diagram.

If you really want to publish this kind of information as a diagram, I recommend automatically generating the diagram using static analysis tools as part of your build process.

We'll look at how you can use diagramming at a code level in Chapter 9, Design and Refactor Your Applications, on page 93, later.

Leverage Flowcharts for Complex Flows

When creating the C4 model, we used Mermaid's Flowchart to do so, as it's the best fit for the job from the available Mermaid diagram types. However, we can use flowcharts for other purposes.

The most obvious choice is, of course, a flowchart to draw out a complex flow. For example, at a former workplace I worked on a decision engine for loans. As you can imagine, the logic applied to each applicant was complicated, with many branches and decision points, so I used a flowchart to document the requirements before beginning work.

This was invaluable for ensuring there was parity between the business stakeholders' understanding and the engineering team, as the flowchart was nontechnical, so could be used as a point of discussion for the initial requirements and in future to ensure changes were being made as expected.

In the prior chapter we used sequence diagrams to model application flows. I find these are better than flowcharts for interactions between systems or classes as they're a little more succinct. However, they don't handle branching logic as well, or highlighting subroutines, so if you find your sequence diagram is getting unwieldly, try a flowchart instead.

What You've Learned

In this chapter, we first covered how to document components within our containers. Keep in mind, not all systems need a component diagram, so only use them when you feel it adds real value. Secondly, we looked at code diagrams, which I don't recommend creating yourself, as they will become rapidly out-of-date.

That's the final chapter on modeling architecture with the C4 model. In the next chapter we'll move into the lowest level in our architecture, the database, and show how we can use diagramming to help design database schemas.

## CHAPTER 7

Design Database Schemas

We've just finished creating C4 diagrams to model the architecture for your system, and as part of that modeling the chances are your system needs some form of persistence. These days, there are many options available to persist your data, but the most common is still some form of database. Whether that be relational (for example, Postgres), document (for example, MongoDB), or other, you should be using schemas to structure your data so it's clear what is stored where and that data is accurate and reliable.

In the majority of systems you work on, you'll likely have a need to store data somewhere. In the first chapter, we modeled the domain we are working in. In this chapter, you'll learn how to design database schemas to support persisting at least parts of that domain. You may not need to persist much of the domain, but the chances are you need to persist something.

While it's definitely possible that the domain entities you defined map one-to-one to entities in the database (such as tables), this isn't always the case. When undertaking a domain modeling exercise, it's important to not think of it in terms of how you would store it in the database. This isn't a book on writing clean code, but a key concept for any engineer to learn is the separation of concerns. In this case, we're separating the concerns of the domain from that of the persistence. In an ideal world, the domain will not know how it's persisted.

A common example of why the domain will differ from the persistence is they have different roles and different responsibilities. The domain is responsible for representing the core concepts of the business, including entities and business logic, whereas the database layer is there to store state in a robust, performant manner. The domain layer doesn't care about how quickly a given row can be looked up from the database, but the database layer certainly does.

Entity Definition in This Chapter

It might be confusing to see the word *entity* used to mean two different things. In the domain modeling chapters, it meant a domain entity. In this chapter, it means an entity in the database, such as a database table. The reason it's called an entity, and not a table, is a table is software-specific. If you were using MongoDB, for example, there would be no tables; instead they're called collections.

For clarity, any use of the word entity in this chapter, unless otherwise specified, relates to an entity in the database.

Let's use an e-commerce store as an example—say we have a Cart which contains many Items. We may choose to have an entity for the cart and an entity for the items, but we may also choose to have a single cart entity that contains the items as JSON in a column. It may evolve from one to the other as the demands of the system change. The power of separating these concerns is that changing it shouldn't impact the domain—the domain will still have classes representing the cart and items.

I'm making this point in this book to ensure that when you undertake each exercise—the domain modeling and the database design—there does not need to be parity between the two. They will likely look different and require different considerations, and it's important to consider both when designing any solutions.

Use Entity Relationship Diagrams

Now that you understand the difference between domain modeling and database design, we can start to design the database schemas. Similarly to other chapters in this book, Mermaid has a specific diagram available for designing database schemas.

A common diagram for designing database schemas is called an entity relationship diagram (ERD). As previously mentioned, the entities are database objects such as tables, not to be confused with domain entities. Its purpose is to define the database schemas for those entities, such as their fields and data types, as well as how the entities link together. ERDs are most commonly used with relational databases but can be used with document databases too, such as representing collections in MongoDB.

I chose to tackle the schema design after I've defined the architecture, as I then know what services are going to exist and where each domain entity, and its respective data, will be stored. I found when considering the ERD before the system architecture that the underlying data model was driving my architecture. However, it's entirely plausible that when you come to design your database schema, you realize the makeup of your services is problematic in terms of the data each one needs. Perhaps Service A and Service B both need to access the same data a lot, so you choose to combine them. Software architecture is iterative, so never be afraid to go back and question your decisions, using the diagrams to validate any decisions.

Unlike the domain model or C4 model, which should be regularly updated, I find ERDs have a different life cycle—I call them snapshot diagrams. I've found three main scenarios where I use them:

1. When writing an architecture decision record (ADR) for a brand-new service, I may optionally include an ERD to show a *snapshot* of the database design at that point in time.

2. When making significant schema changes to an existing service, it's often helpful to include a *snapshot* of the database schema to help understand in the future why that decision was made. This might be another ADR or included on PRs that make the change.

3. When making small schema changes, it can be helpful to draw out the change visually to quickly see if the change makes sense or to simply help explain the change to a colleague.

I've highlighted the word *snapshot* in the preceding list, as that's what it should be in my opinion. The database is going to evolve, and the ERD will get out-of-date. You don't necessarily need to update the ERD every time you update the database schema, because the schemas themselves are the source of truth. However, it can be very useful to include snapshots of what the database schemas looked like at that point in time to aid with rationalizing changes or explaining changes to others. Whenever I use an ERD, I make sure to call out that it's simply a snapshot, and not the source of truth.

As we will soon see, the functionality provided by an ERD is similar to that of a class diagram. However, I'll highlight key differences as we go through, and I'll explain why we didn't create our domain model using an ERD.

Define Our First Entity

Where you start is entirely up to you, as the schemas for the entities will evolve as you add them or you change the way in which you persist entities.

If you're not sure, always start with the most important domain entities and work your way through the relationships until you've finished.

We'll be defining an ERD for our entire domain model, which you might end up doing if you have a monolith, but typically you define an ERD for a given service that implements part of your domain model, such as in a microservices architecture.

Automatically Exporting ERDs

I wouldn't create an ERD for the entire enterprise you work in. If you really want that view, tools are available that can do that for you. MySQL Workbench, for example, allows you to export an ERD from the database schemas.

It won't produce you a Mermaid diagram, just an image, but it can be useful to get a view of every entity and its storage across all the company's services.

Let's add the Title entity first:

```
erDiagram
    TITLE {
        int title_id
        string name
        datetime release_date
    }
```

When rendered with Mermaid, it looks like this:

TITLE	
int	title_id
string	name
datetime	release_date

Delving into this line by line, the first tells Mermaid this is an entity relationship diagram. The remaining lines define the TITLE entity, starting with its name (which is always in capitals) and a curly bracket ({), which tells Mermaid we want to define fields.

Between the curly brackets, we can define one column per line. First, we define the type for the field, followed by the name of the field. In our case, we've defined TITLE with an ID, name, and release date.

That's our first entity defined! But an entity on its own isn't much use, so let's look at how we can define relationships between entities.

Relate Entities

Now that we know how to define entities, we can start to relate them to one another. In our domain model, we determined that a Title could be one of many types: TV Show, Short, and Film. Therefore, we need to store those types and allow a Title to reference a type. Our updated Mermaid definition looks like so:

```
erDiagram
    TITLE {
        int title_id
        int type_id
        string name
        datetime release_date
    }

    TITLE_TYPE {
        int type_id
        string type
    }

    TITLE }|--|| TITLE_TYPE: has
```

I'll highlight a few changes here. Firstly, we add a second entity to represent the types a title can have. Secondly, we add a type_id field on the Title entity that will be used to link the title to a type.

Finally, we define a relationship between TITLE and TITLE_TYPE. Defining relationships follows this format:

```
ENTITY_NAME_1 CARDINALITY--CARDINALITY ENTITY_NAME_2:
```

Cardinality can be one of four types. We'll cover all four as we add entities, but for now || means "exactly one," and }| means "one-to-many." Similarly to a class diagram, such as the one we used for our domain model, you define the cardinality for a given entity on the opposite side to the entity itself. Therefore, in the example format, the cardinality for ENTITY_NAME_1 is after the two hyphens.

One of the reasons I don't recommend ERDs for domain modeling is the way in which cardinalities are displayed. They use what's called crow's feet, which I don't find particularly intuitive, especially when compared to the numeric format used on class diagrams, which are easy for anyone to understand at a glance. That's one reason why we didn't use an ERD for our domain model.

Lastly, all the syntax used for relationships can be flipped so they can be used on either side of the relationship. Instead of how I defined the preceding relationship, you could define it like so:

```
TITLE_TYPE ||--|{ TITLE: has
```

If we generate the diagram now, this is how it looks:

As you can see, a cardinality of exactly one is represented as two horizontal lines, while one-to-many is represented by three lines in the rough shape of an arrow. In ERDs, the "many" options (of which we'll cover another later) are often called crow's feet due to how they look, and in the case of one-to-many the single horizontal line dictates there must be at least one. In essence, this means the existence of a record is mandatory when it is marked as one-to-many.

Add Zero-to-Many Relationships

We covered how to display mandatory records, but what about optional records?

This is where zero-to-many relationships come in. In the case of Streamy, a title's genre is optional, so let's add that to our ERD, like so:

```
erDiagram
    TITLE {
        int title_id
        int type_id
        string name
        datetime release_date
    }
```

```
TITLE_TYPE {
    int type_id
    string type
}
GENRE {
    int genre_id PK
    string name
}
TITLE_GENRE {
    int title_id
    int genre_id
}
TITLE }|--|| TITLE_TYPE: has
TITLE ||--o{ TITLE_GENRE: "belongs to"

TITLE_GENRE }o--|| GENRE: references
```

When rendered, we can see the crow's feet again to show a many relationship between the TITLE and TITLE_GENRE entities, but this time an empty circle is displayed instead of a horizontal line to denote that there may or may not be records related between the entities.

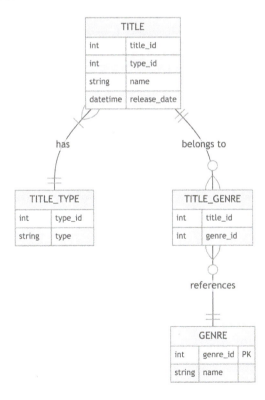

In terms of Mermaid syntax, zero-to-many cardinalities are represented similarly to one-to-many, except instead of a horizontal line, it's the letter o. Therefore, the full notation is o{. One other thing to note is labels that contain multiple words need to be wrapped in double quotes, which you can see in the preceding example.

Earlier, we discussed how the database schema represented by the ERD will likely differ from the domain model shown in the class diagram. We can start to see this play out in our ERD, where we do have TITLE and GENRE. However, we need additional entities that don't feature in the domain model, such as TITLE_GENRE, which is allowing a title to have multiple genres and genres to have multiple titles. If you're familiar with databases, this is often referred to as a join entity.

We can now add zero-to-many relationships to our ERD, along with one-to-many. These kinds of relationships often rely on keys, so how do we add those to our diagram?

Enrich Schemas with Keys

In our ERD so far, we can see there are columns defined to enable entities to be linked together. In some ERDs you may see these columns omitted, as the relationships implicitly show there must be columns present, in the form of foreign keys, to link the entities. However, I'm a fan of generally being explicit, so I choose to add the columns.

Along the same line of thought, we can explicitly mark columns as primary keys or foreign keys where appropriate. Adding keys is achieved by adding a third parameter when defining a column, with only PK (primary key) or FK (foreign key) being allowed.

Adding keys to the TITLE_GENRE entity looks like so:

```
TITLE_GENRE {
    int title_id PK
    int genre_id PK
}
```

I recommend always adding keys to your entities, so it's clear to everyone that those keys exist and how two entities are linked. To aid readability, I always put the primary key columns first, so it's clear to everyone reading what makes a row unique.

You may have noticed we only defined primary keys, but both title_id and genre_id would be foreign keys too. Unfortunately, Mermaid doesn't support specifying both PK and FK in the same parameter.

Luckily, in the event we need both, we can make use of comments to specify foreign keys. Let's look at how to do that next.

Comment Your Columns

Similarly to how we added an extra parameter for keys, there's one final parameter reserved for column comments. They're completely optional but can be handy if you need to explain something about a particular column—such as specifying a foreign key. Here's what it looks like in Mermaid if we add a comment to specify the missing foreign keys from the TITLE_GENRE entity:

```
TITLE_GENRE {
    int title_id PK "FK"
    int genre_id PK "FK"
}
```

If we add the remaining missing keys, and comments where necessary, our ERD looks like this:

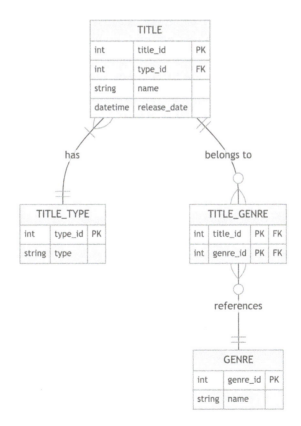

I think this is a good compromise, and it renders nicely. Don't be afraid to add both a foreign key and additional comments to the same column, such as FK. Your comment here.

Now that we've added all the keys, we have one more relationship type to discuss. So far, we've added exactly one, zero-to-many, and one-to-many relationships to our diagrams. Let's look at this last one.

Define Zero-or-One Relationships

The final type of relationship we can add to an ERD is zero-or-one. This type of relationship is exactly as it sounds and should be used in cases where there might be a relationship between two entities, but if there is, there's only at most one.

An example outside of Streamy might be a government car registration website, where a car would have a zero-or-one relationship to an owner, as not all cars have owners at all times.

Within Streamy, a Review can be made against a title, episode, or season. Therefore, a Review has a zero-or-one relationship with all three of those, as it can only be made against one of the three. In technical terms, you can think of a zero-or-one relationship as a foreign key that is nullable.

Let's add REVIEW and SEASON to our ERD and add their respective relationships to other entities:

```
erDiagram
    TITLE {
        int title_id PK
        int type_id FK
        string name
        datetime release_date
    }
    TITLE_TYPE {
        int type_id PK
        string type
    }
    GENRE {
        int genre_id PK
        string name
    }
    TITLE_GENRE {
        int title_id PK "FK"
        int genre_id PK "FK"
    }
```

```
SEASON {
    int season_id PK
    int title_id FK
    int season_number
    date release_year
}
REVIEW {
    int review_id PK
    int title_id FK
    int season_id FK
    string review_by
    datetime review_date
    string review_text
}
TITLE }|--|| TITLE_TYPE: has
TITLE ||--o{ TITLE_GENRE: "belongs to"
TITLE ||--|{ SEASON: contains

TITLE_GENRE }o--|| GENRE: references

REVIEW }o--o| TITLE: "made against"
REVIEW }o--o| SEASON: "made against"
```

Zero-or-one relationships are shown using o|, and when rendered by Mermaid, they are shown as a circle followed by a horizontal line. I also added SEASON to the ERD, which uses syntax you learned already. What it looks like is shown on page 80.

We've now covered all the possible relationship types in an ERD! We've always separated the cardinalities with two hyphens, but those hyphens have a meaning, so let's discuss more about them.

Remembering ERD Relationship Syntax

When defining a relationship from one entity to another, only three characters are used:

- Zero, represented by an o.
- One, represented by a |.
- Many, represented by a {.

That makes ERDs one of the simpler diagrams in terms of syntax, with each relationship definition using one of these characters to define the minimum and one to define the maximum for that relationship. For example, o{ translates to zero (minimum) to many (maximum). The maximum value is always closest to the entity name when defining a relationship.

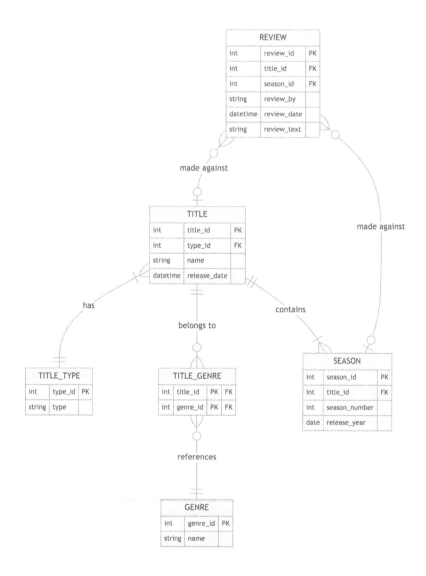

Describe Non-identifying Relationships

All relationships can either be identifying or non-identifying. In an ERD, this is the way to detail whether or not two entities can exist independently of one another. It can be tricky to determine independence, so there's a clear way in database terms to decide whether a relationship is identifying or non-identifying.

In technical terms, we can use the keys between entities to decide between identifying and non-identifying. If the primary key of the parent entity is included in the primary key of a child entity, it's an identifying relationship. Therefore, if the parent entity's primary key is not included in the child entity's primary key, it's non-identifying.

So far, all relationships we defined used identifying syntax, which is two hyphens between the cardinality of each entity. If we want to mark a relationship as non-identifying, we simply change those two hyphens to two dots.

Let's update the ERD, as the majority of the relationships we've added so far are identifying. The only ones not are these:

- TITLE and TITLE_GENRE
- TITLE_GENRE and GENRE

Therefore, to update TITLE and TITLE_TYPE to be non-identifying, we can do the following:

```
TITLE }|..|| TITLE_TYPE: has
```

Note the change between the two relationship definitions—it's now two dots instead of two hyphens.

When rendered with Mermaid, non-identifying relationships are shown using a dashed line rather than a solid line. If we update all the other relationships to be non-identifying, our ERD now looks like this:

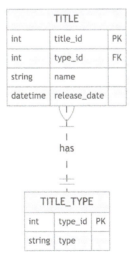

In a larger application, a classic example of where you'd see more identifying relationships is where a domain entity is broken down into many database entities. For instance, you might store user data and have a USER entity. However, storing all the data in one entity might mean the entity becomes huge in terms of size on disk and you're constantly adding columns to it. As someone that's worked on a database where columns were constantly added to the main user entity, and adding columns took hours due to the size of the entity, I can say that you definitely want to break it up.

Therefore, you might have a series of entities, such as USER_ADDRESS, USER_PHONE_NUMBER, and USER_EMAIL. This approach has other benefits, such as easily being able to store data such as address history easily.

That covers non-identifying relationships! You've now learned all the syntax for an ERD, but before it's over to you to create your own ERD, let's first complete the entity relationship diagram for Streamy.

Finalize Streamy's ERD

That sums up the functionality available to us when creating entity relationship diagrams. Just to round out the diagram, here's the final Mermaid markup for the missing domain entities we defined in our domain model, which uses syntax you already learned. Once again, I've signed this diagram off as complete by adding a title to finish it:

```
---
title: Streamy Entity Relationship Diagram
---
erDiagram
    TITLE {
        int title_id PK
        int type_id FK
        string name
        datetime release_date
    }

    TITLE_TYPE {
        int type_id PK
        string type
    }

    ACTOR {
        int actor_id PK
        string name
        date date_of_birth
    }
```

```
TITLE_ACTOR {
    int title_id PK "FK"
    int actor_id PK "FK"
}
GENRE {
    int genre_id PK
    string name
}
TITLE_GENRE {
    int title_id PK "FK"
    int genre_id PK "FK"
}
EPISODE {
    int episode_id PK
    int season_id FK
    string name
    int season_number
    int episode_number
    datetime release_date
}
SEASON {
    int season_id PK
    int title_id FK
    int season_number
    date release_year
}
REVIEW {
    int review_id PK
    int title_id FK
    int episode_id FK
    int season_id FK
    string review_by
    datetime review_date
    string review_text
}
TITLE }|..|| TITLE_TYPE: has
TITLE ||--o{ TITLE_GENRE: "belongs to"
TITLE ||--|{ TITLE_ACTOR: features
TITLE ||..|{ SEASON: contains

TITLE_GENRE }o--|| GENRE: references

TITLE_ACTOR }|--|| ACTOR: references

EPISODE }|..|| SEASON: contains

REVIEW }o..o| TITLE: "made against"
REVIEW }o..o| EPISODE: "made against"
REVIEW }o..o| SEASON: "made against"
```

And here's how it looks when rendered using Mermaid:

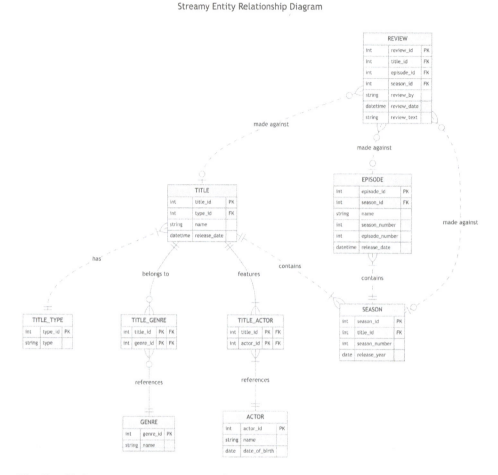

Streamy Entity Relationship Diagram

That's all there is to it, in terms of an ERD. You're now ready to create your own ERD, so let's get to it!

Design Your Database Schema

That rounds out everything there is to know about ERDs in Mermaid. Now it's your turn to create your own ERD for one of your projects.

Create an ERD diagram, using what we've covered in this chapter. Try to pick a project with a varied schema, so that you can try to include all of the functionality you've learned. It doesn't need to be huge or complex, but try to include identifying and non-identifying relationships, primary keys and foreign keys, and varying cardinalities.

If you can't think of a project that's suitable, or perhaps you've never worked on relational databases much, feel free to pick a well-known website you use regularly. Using what they display on their website, try to build an ERD that would underpin their website.

What You've Learned

In this chapter, you learned how to create an entity relationship diagram to design and detail database schemas. As part of creating one, we covered the differences between entities in a domain model and entities in an ERD: entities in the domain model represent concepts in the business, and entities in the ERD represent database entities. We also discussed how to define the entities, their columns, types, keys, and any comments. This can be achieved using syntax similar to the following:

```
TITLE {
    int id PK
    int type_id FK "this is a comment"
    string name
    datetime release_date
}
```

Entities on their own don't provide much value, so we covered how to relate entities using four different types of relationship: one-to-many (|{), zero-to-many (o{), one-to-one (||), and zero-or-one (o|).

Finally, we covered identifying and non-identifying relationships: identifying means one entity cannot exist without another, and non-identifying means they can exist independent of one another. In Mermaid, we show identifying with -- between the cardinality, and .. for non-identifying.

That pretty much covers all the diagrams that would be useful when designing a service! That's not all though—I want to show you one more use case for diagramming: when designing and refactoring code, which we'll cover in the next chapter, followed by how we can ensure diagrams are kept up-to-date and relevant.

## CHAPTER 8

Visualize Code Flows

In the last chapter, Chapter 7, Design Database Schemas, on page 69, we produced what I would class as a snapshot diagram in the form of an entity relationship diagram. As opposed to the diagrams such as the domain model or C4 diagrams, snapshot diagrams are used to visualize something in that moment. We'll continue exploring snapshot diagrams in this chapter with a very different use case: designing and refactoring code.

You might think you don't need diagrams for that purpose—after all, you have your IDE, right?

I've found it to be extremely useful to use diagrams in some use cases when working directly with code. A common one I come across is explaining how several classes interact with each other to a colleague. The IDE, especially if you're unfamiliar with the codebase, is full of distractions and misdirection. Furthermore, if that colleague is trying to work on that area of the codebase and doesn't understand it, perhaps the raw code isn't the right lens with which to help them.

Another example would be when, instead of trying to understand how classes interact in terms of sequence, you want to understand dependencies between classes. The number of dependencies and the dependency tree can be useful tools to visualize to understand where there might be code to improve.

In both cases, that's where Mermaid comes in. You may have already twigged the types of diagram we can use for each use case, as we already covered them, just for different use cases.

For the first example, understanding interactions between classes, we can use a sequence diagram. We last used a sequence diagram in Chapter 3, Visualize Application and User Flows, on page 23, to understand application flows, but we can do the same for code with a few extra bits of syntax to help us.

For the second example, understanding dependencies between classes, we can use a class diagram. We'll look at that in the next chapter: Chapter 9, Design and Refactor Your Applications, on page 93. At the very start of the book, in Chapter 1, Document Your Domain, on page 1, we used a class diagram to cover creating a domain model. Similarly to sequence diagrams, we didn't cover all the syntax for class diagrams though, such as defining properties and methods, as that wasn't needed for a domain model. However, for refactoring code, it's incredibly useful, so we'll learn how to define those on a class diagram in that chapter.

These next two chapters go hand in hand and approach the same use case from two different angles.

Streamy was blessed by a successful launch, but it didn't come for free. As is common, to meet deadlines some corners were cut, and some tech debt was taken on board. That tech debt now needs to be paid, so let's start with the first example!

Use Sequence Diagrams to Understand Class Interactions

The use cases for sequence diagrams are almost endless in terms of understanding the interactions of different elements in a flow. Earlier, in Chapter 3, Visualize Application and User Flows, on page 23, we used one to model an application flow to understand how a user can sign up at Streamy. That was a high-level flow, looking at interactions between different containers.

In this chapter, we'll zoom in a little on one of the interactions in that sequence diagram: an HTTP POST from the user's browser to the user service. This endpoint creates a new user within the system along with some additional behavior such as publishing an event to Kafka and sending the user a welcome email.

We're using a sequence diagram for the same purpose as before, but the lens through which we're viewing something is much more zoomed in. We're no longer at a high level, but we still need to understand the interactions between elements in a flow. When it comes to code, this is not always straightforward, especially if you're working on a large legacy system, and in particular a monolith. If I can't work out how something fits together, I want to consider a potential refactor, or if I want to design implementing a new feature, I often reach for a sequence diagram to understand the interactions. This works similarly well if a colleague is struggling to grasp how a set of classes interact.

The majority of the syntax will be familiar to you already, so we're going to jump straight into the full example:

```
---
title: POST /users Request Handling
---
sequenceDiagram
    autonumber

    participant UserController
    participant CreateUserService
    participant UserModel
    participant SendWelcomeEmailService
    participant Kafka

    UserController->>+CreateUserService: call
    CreateUserService->>UserModel: find_users_by_email
    UserModel-->>CreateUserService: array of Users

    loop
        CreateUserService->>CreateUserService: check_active_users
    end

    CreateUserService->>UserModel: create_user
    UserModel-->>CreateUserService: User

    par
        CreateUserService->>SendWelcomeEmailService: send_welcome_email
        SendWelcomeEmailService-->>CreateUserService: boolean

        CreateUserService->>Kafka: publish_user_created_event
        Kafka-->>CreateUserService: boolean
    end

    CreateUserService-->>-UserController: User
```

Don't get too hung up on the architecture of the code or the names—I'm not suggesting you write classes like this—but it gives you a simple idea of how you can model class interactions using sequence diagrams. This only took me ten minutes to put together—a lot quicker than writing the code out first and then realizing there's a problem! There's no guarantee that because you draw it out, it's going to work, but the investment in doing so is small and can often help you consider the approach quickly and easily before writing actual code.

Just keep in mind that sequence diagrams are high level and are not good at providing any more than a basic level of detail. They should only be used for displaying interactions, with more detailed information such as properties and methods saved for a class diagram, which we'll cover later in this chapter.

Here's how the diagram looks once generated:

POST /users Request Handling

The sequence itself is simple, essentially detailing the interactions required between classes. You can describe the interactions using plain English, but I prefer to use method names, and types in the returns. A lot of this should be familiar, such as using autonumber to add numbers to the interactions, solid lines for the start of an interaction, and dotted lines to indicate returns for an interaction. I'm also making use of an activation for the entirety of the CreateUserService logic to highlight just how much work is happening in that one request from the controller.

A couple of new pieces of syntax, which we haven't covered yet, are particularly useful for modeling class interactions. Let's touch on those next.

Define Loops

One of the most common things to do in any programming language is to iterate over a piece of data, typically using a loop. In our example here, we need to loop over the results of a query to find users by email to determine if any are active. It's detailed on the sequence diagram like so:

```
loop
    CreateUserService->CreateUserService: check_active_users
end
```

The syntax is simple: you put anything that is happening in a loop within loop and end, and Mermaid will create a clear indication on the diagram that this is a loop. In this contrived example, there can be multiple users with the same email, but only one can be active at any one time. In reality, you'd almost certainly check for active accounts when calling the model, but for the purpose of showing how a loop can be used, this works well to make the service do it.

Within the loop and end you can use any valid Mermaid you like—for example, you can add interactions between participants or even show branching logic using alt, such as in Show Branching Logic, on page 26.

That's it for loops, and almost finishes the section on sequence diagrams, but first we have one more piece of functionality to uncover: parallelization.

Show Parallel Processes

So far, our sequence diagram is sequential. Each interaction in the sequence is happening one after the other, in a procedural manner. However, in the real world, that's not always the case. Often, a process's performance can be improved through parallelizing parts of the flow.

We can show this with Mermaid too! Adding parallel sections is done like this:

```
par
    CreateUserService->>SendWelcomeEmailService: send_welcome_email
    SendWelcomeEmailService-->>CreateUserService: boolean

    CreateUserService->>Kafka: publish_user_created_event
    Kafka-->>CreateUserService: boolean
end
```

When rendered, it looks almost identical to a loop, with just a change in label in the top left. Any interactions that start within the par and end are happening in parallel. In this example, we're sending the welcome email to new Streamy customers and publishing a user created event to Kafka in parallel. I'm not suggesting that's a good approach from a code perspective, but it serves the purpose of showing interactions happening in parallel.

Similarly to the loop, you can put any valid Mermaid in the parallel block—you can even nest a parallel block inside a parallel block if subsequent calls are also parallelized.

That covers everything new in the sequence diagram, and we now have a good high-level overview of how the code is working. Generally, I use sequence diagrams at a code level in two ways:

1. To understand the interactions between classes, in particular to understand how the code is working for a given process. In this example, we now understand how the code fits together to create a new user.

2. To identify possible inefficiencies in the process or interactions that don't make sense. For example, checking for active users in the CreateUserService doesn't make any sense—it should be moved into the UserModel and done as part of the query. Similarly, we're sending the email and publishing an event in parallel, so are the gains in performance worth the complexity of handling parallelization?

Ultimately, you can't begin to work on or improve code until you understand it. That's exactly where a sequence diagram comes in and where I've found the most value when working with my colleagues over the years.

What You've Learned

This was a small but important chapter. I've lost count of the number of times I, or my colleagues, have used a sequence diagram to understand how an area of the codebase works. Next time you or a colleague is having trouble understanding an area of the codebase, give it a try and see if it helps you as much as it helps me.

The majority of the Mermaid syntax was familiar from prior chapters, in particular Chapter 3, Visualize Application and User Flows, on page 23. We did, however, cover how to define loops, wrapping any code that is looped inside of loop and end. Secondly, we discussed how to define parallel code paths, using par and end. Any code between par and end will be executed in parallel.

Now that we understand the code at a high level, we might want to take a closer look at the classes themselves. As the sequence diagram is just a high-level view, we can use a class diagram to get a better view of the individual classes as well as their dependencies. That's exactly what we'll do in the next chapter.

## CHAPTER 9

Design and Refactor Your Applications

In the prior chapter, we looked at a series of classes and how they interact to create a new user within a given system. In this chapter we're going to build upon that example, but from a different angle. We now understand the order in which code is executed, but that's only one piece of the puzzle. While visualizing the execution order is valuable to understand the sequence of events for a given process, we also need to understand the dependencies of the classes.

You may be thinking you can infer the dependencies by looking at the sequence diagram, and in some cases that's true. However, a sequence diagram only shows a basic view of the world. Looking at the sequence diagram, we may assume that the UserController has a direct dependency on the CreateUserSerivce. At a code level, that might not be true—we'll see why later in the chapter. Furthermore, it only shows the public methods called between classes. It doesn't show any private methods, nor properties, and it doesn't go into detail around data types, such as User in this example.

When considering changes to code, one diagram I regularly reach for to get all of this information in one place is a class diagram. It gives you a different view to a sequence diagram and a different view to the one you get in your editor. When looking at code in an editor, you see it somewhat in a vacuum. You can see a single class and its dependencies, maybe a couple of classes if you split your editor windows, but visually it can be hard to clearly see the dependencies for an area of the codebase.

That's where I reach for a class diagram. I don't do it every time I write code—far from it. If I'm doing a small refactor, extracting a method for example, it's wasteful to create a diagram. However, if I'm doing a larger refactor, particularly if I'm adding a new feature and want to refactor before, I often want to see the dependencies and methods at play first. You can certainly do it in your editor, but I guarantee you'll spend a lot of time jumping back and forth between classes, forgetting what class depended on another. A class diagram can be created in no time, so I find in the long run it pays dividends to take the time to draw one.

Exporting Class Diagrams

 In lots of languages, in particular statically typed languages such as Java and C#, it's possible to export class diagrams automatically. This is definitely quicker than drawing it with Mermaid and in some cases might be all you need. However, it won't be editable, as it will just be an image, so won't fit all use cases, as we'll soon see.

To identify some possible improvements to the code, let's start by drawing the class diagram!

Define Classes

We already used a class diagram in Chapter 1, Document Your Domain, on page 1; however, there's more functionality available that we're yet to cover. We're going to create a class diagram to represent the classes used in the sequence diagram.

Let's start by adding two classes, the UserController and the CreateUserService:

```
classDiagram
    class UserController {
        -CreateUserService _createUserService
        +UserController(CreateUserService createUserService)
        +Create(string email, string username) User
    }
    class CreateUserService {
        -UserModel _userModel
        -SendWelcomeEmailService _sendWelcomeEmailService
        -Kafka _kafka
        +CreateUserService(UserModel um, SendWelcomeEmailService es, Kafka k)
        +Call(string email, string username) User
        -CheckActiveUsers(List~User~ users) bool
    }
```

As you already know, the first line informs Mermaid we're creating a class diagram, but there's new syntax in the remainder of the markup.

Firstly, we explicitly define classes in a class diagram. We didn't need to do this in the domain model, because we weren't interested in properties or methods, so we could simply describe the relationships. However, as we're now at the code level, we definitely want to describe the properties and methods on each class. In the actual code, I wouldn't use acronyms for parameter names such as you see for CreateUserService—I've used shorthand just to keep it on one line in the book.

In Mermaid, this is done using the following syntax:

```
class ClassName {
    -PropertyType propertyName
    +MethodName(MethodParamType methodParam) ReturnType
}
```

I find the syntax very readable and simple to write. For each class we must explicitly define it and give it a name, as per the first line. Following the name, we can define an unlimited number of properties, defining the type and name of the property for each one. After we've defined properties, we can define methods. We differentiate properties from methods by adding () to the end of the method names, with any parameters and their respective types defined within the brackets. Finally, we define the return type of methods after the closing circular bracket.

One other piece of information we define is the visibility of a property or method. That's defined in Mermaid using - (private) or + (public) before the property or method.

We use the same syntax to define the CreateUserService class. When rendered, this is how classes and their properties and methods are displayed:

As you can see, it renders each class as its own box. Within each box is the class's name, followed by any properties, and lastly, the methods belonging to that class. It's a clear way to see what's going on in each class but doesn't show how classes relate to one another.

For that, we need to define relationships, similarly to when we created the domain model.

Show Dependencies with Relationships

Now that we've got two classes defined, we can add a relationship between them. The types of relationships you learned when domain modeling won't be useful here, as the domain model doesn't need to show code-level dependencies. Adding a dependency is simple in Mermaid, so let's add a dependency between the UserController and the CreateUserService:

```
UserController ..> CreateUserService: depends on
```

Simple, right?

We define a dependency using ..>, with the arrow pointing to the dependent. While optional, I always recommend adding a label to a description too. In the case of a class diagram, I describe the type of relationship (for example, depends on, inherits from, and so on), as the chances are not everyone will be familiar with Mermaid or UML syntax, so the label ensures everyone knows exactly what the arrow represents.

That's all the new syntax we need to complete the class diagram, so here's the full Mermaid markup:

```
classDiagram
    class UserController {
        -CreateUserService _createUserService
        +UserController(CreateUserService createUserService)
        +Create(string email, string username) User
    }
    class CreateUserService {
        -UserModel _userModel
        -SendWelcomeEmailService _sendWelcomeEmailService
        -Kafka _kafka
        +CreateUserService(UserModel um, SendWelcomeEmailService es, Kafka k)
        +Call(string email, string username) User
        -CheckActiveUsers(List~User~ users) bool
    }
    class UserModel {
        +FindUsersByEmail(string email) List~User~
        +CreateUser(string email, string username) User
    }
    class User {
        +int UserId
        +string Username
        +string Email
    }
```

```
class SendWelcomeEmailService {
    +Call(string email, string username) bool
}
class Kafka {
    +PublishUserCreatedEvent(string email, string username) bool
}
UserController ..> CreateUserService: depends on
CreateUserService ..> UserModel: depends on
UserModel ..> User: depends on
CreateUserService ..> SendWelcomeEmailService: depends on
CreateUserService ..> Kafka: depends on
```

Mermaid renders a dependency as a dashed line with a small, nonsolid arrowhead. Let's see what that looks like, and how all the dependencies play out:

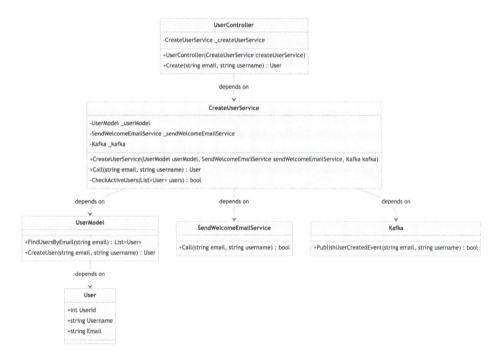

When combined with the sequence diagram, we now have an excellent overview of *how* classes interact and in what order, and thanks to the class diagram, we get a good view of the structure of the classes, and their dependencies.

I often play around with the classes and dependencies as a tool to use for refactoring, before touching any code—so what improvements could we make to the code?

Refactor the Classes

Before we get into the refactoring aspect, when I was planning this chapter, I initially planned to use two separate examples for the sequence diagram and the class diagram. I thought there was no way, in the small number of interactions and classes, there would be any examples of refactoring to use!

Even after years of diagramming, it still continues to amaze me what insights it can give so quickly, and often surprisingly. Because, as it turns out, when I drew this class diagram, I found several improvements we could make. Let's look at the first one.

Introduce a Request Class

As this isn't a book on refactoring, but a book on diagramming, I won't spend too long looking at the possible refactors. However, I think it's a good way to demonstrate the kinds of insights you can gain from creating these diagrams.

The first code smell I noticed was several of the classes containing the same parameters, but each time we're passing the parameters individually as primitive types (for example, string, integer, and so on). The parameters in this example are email and username, but in reality there are likely more to create a user, such as their name, phone number, and address. I kept the parameters short for readability, but even when there are just two, we're still passing them around together a lot, and we can definitely find a better way to represent them.

This is one of the common code smells that a lot of automated code analysis tools identify these days. If we had more parameters, it would probably be *long parameter list*, but as we only have two, it's likely a *data clump*. In essence, you can identify this code smell when you see the same pieces of data passed together but as separate parameters.

The fix is easy: we create a class to group the data points and pass that in the method signature instead. Here's how that looks if we update our Mermaid to introduce this new class:

```
classDiagram
    class UserController {
        -CreateUserService _createUserService
        +UserController(CreateUserService createUserService)
        +Create(string email, string username) User
    }
```

```
class CreateUserRequest {
    +string Email
    +string Username

    +Validate() bool
}
class CreateUserService {
    -UserModel _userModel
    -SendWelcomeEmailService _sendWelcomeEmailService
    -Kafka _kafka
    +CreateUserService(UserModel um, SendWelcomeEmailService es, Kafka k)
    +Call(CreateUserRequest createUserRequest) User
    -CheckActiveUsers(List~User~ users) bool
}
class UserModel {
    +FindUsersByEmail(string email) List~User~
    +CreateUser(string email, string username) User
}
class User {
    +int UserId
    +string Username
    +string Email
}
class SendWelcomeEmailService {
    +Call(User user) bool
}
class Kafka {
    +PublishUserCreatedEvent(User User) bool
}
UserController ..> CreateUserRequest: depends on
UserController ..> CreateUserService: depends on
CreateUserService ..> UserModel: depends on
UserModel ..> User: depends on
CreateUserService ..> SendWelcomeEmailService: depends on
CreateUserService ..> Kafka: depends on
```

If we render the updated Mermaid markup, our class diagram now looks like the diagram shown on page 100.

As you can see, the UserController now has an extra dependency in the form of the CreateUserRequest class. The request class itself has two public properties representing the data needed to create a user, as well as a validate method to ensure the data is accurate.

That wasn't the only change though. We needed to update the CreateUserService's Call method to now accept the new class instead of the individual parameters.

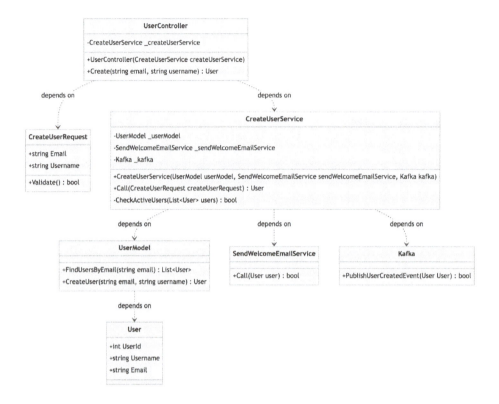

The keen-eyed of you might've noticed some other changes, but can you spot another similar refactoring I added at the same time?

That's right, instead of passing individual parameters to the SendWelcomeEmailService and Kafka classes, we're now passing an instance of the User class, which eliminates the code smell there too. If we wanted, we could go one step further and pass an instance of User to the UserModel, which it then uses to persist to the database. However, that's enough on this aspect of refactoring to demonstrate the point.

I want to cover one more refactor, and this one is a large one. We'll also need some new Mermaid syntax to achieve it!

Define Interfaces

You may have noticed that all of the classes depend on concrete implementations. This isn't a book on writing clean code, so I don't want to go into too much detail, but relying on concrete classes leads to tight coupling between classes. This ultimately makes the code harder to work with, as a change in one class often directly impacts the class it depends on.

A common approach to breaking coupling between classes is to use and rely on interfaces instead of concrete implementations. For those not familiar, interfaces can be seen as defining a contract. They contain no logic; they just define the methods that a class must implement to fulfil that contract. At a code level, that means classes can depend on an interface rather than a concrete class. This in turn breaks the coupling between them, as class A no longer knows about class B—it just knows it will receive an instance of a class that adheres to the interface it depends on.

This is an interesting topic, and a valuable lesson to learn if you're not already familiar, but is beyond the scope of this book. Instead, I highly recommend reading *The Pragmatic Programmer*[1] which covers the topic in far more detail and can do it far more justice than I can in a couple of paragraphs!

I'm not going to add interfaces for every class but will demonstrate by adding one interface. I'm going to add an interface for the CreateUserService, like so:

```
class ICreateUserService {
    <<Interface>>
    +Call(CreateUserRequest createUserRequest) User
}
```

It looks very similar to a class, except we've explicitly annotated the class as an interface using <<Interface>>. There's no restriction on what you can put as an annotation, so feel free to annotate as you see fit. Some other common ones would be Class and Abstract to represent concrete classes and abstract classes, respectively. The naming and segregation of interfaces is another topic well covered in *The Pragmatic Programmer* book.

That defines the interface, but to make use of it we must update the type references in the UserController and CreateUserService and their respective relationships:

```
class UserController {
    <<Class>>
    -ICreateUserService _createUserService
    +UserController(ICreateUserService createUserService)
    +Create(string email, string username) User
}
class ICreateUserService {
    <<Interface>>
    +Call(CreateUserRequest createUserRequest) User
}
```

---

1. https://pragprog.com/titles/tpp20/the-pragmatic-programmer-20th-anniversary-edition/

```
class CreateUserService {
    <<Class>>
    -UserModel _userModel
    -SendWelcomeEmailService _sendWelcomeEmailService
    -Kafka _kafka
    +CreateUserService(UserModel um, SendWelcomeEmailService es, Kafka k)
    +Call(CreateUserRequest createUserRequest) User
    -CheckActiveUsers(List~User~ users) bool
}

UserController ..> ICreateUserService: depends on
CreateUserService ..|> ICreateUserService: implements
```

As always, I'm choosing to be explicit by marking the concrete classes as just that. You could argue it's obsolete, but my counter is it requires little effort to add them for avoidance of doubt.

I've also used a new type of relationship, called a *realization*. You can see it on the last line, with the syntax ..|>. When one element realizes another element, it means it realizes the behavior of the child element. In most cases, this means a class implements the interface it points to.

If I render the full diagram, complete with annotations and the new interface, this is what it looks like:

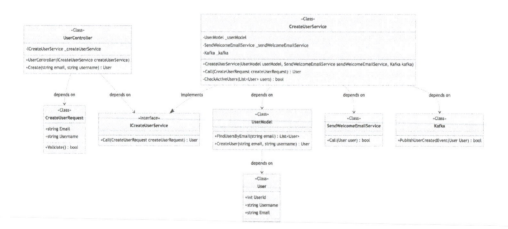

The change is small in terms of markup, but in terms of how we arrange our code, it's hugely impactful for the reasons we touched on in the preceding discussion. Most importantly, we've been able to visually represent the improvement we want to make to the code. Instead of there being a direct dependency between the UserController and CreateUserService, they now know nothing about one another. All the UserController knows is it will be given an instance of a class that implements the interface it needs, and the CreateUserService implements (or realizes, in UML) that interface.

On a code level, this is a big improvement, because the two classes are no longer coupled. However, another benefit of using diagramming for refactoring is for visually demonstrating the improvement to the code. This concept isn't an easy one to grasp, but I find visualizing it makes it much easier for others to understand when I explain the concept. In particular, when I start with the diagram lacking interfaces, and then a colleague can visually see the arrows change, breaking that coupling that existed before, it's often like a light-bulb moment.

We could discuss further refactoring, but that's not the aim of this book, so we'll stop there. An important lesson to take from this chapter, and the book in general, is that while diagramming is incredibly useful for documentation purposes, it has equally powerful uses for learning and collaborating on code changes.

Create a Class Diagram

Once again, it's time for you to get creative!

Find an area of a codebase you work on, and create a class diagram of its dependencies. There should be several classes involved—try to aim for at least five. Make sure you include each class's properties, methods, and relationships.

Once you've drawn it, an optional bonus activity is to try and identify some improvements to the code. If you spot some, try making those changes in the diagram. If you want to go all out, you could turn that improved diagram into reality by making the changes in the code to see the full power of the end-to-end life cycle of refactoring using class diagrams.

What You've Learned

In this chapter, you learned all about leveraging class diagrams to understand dependencies between classes, with the view to use that knowledge to identify potential refactors of the code.

To do so, we covered how to define classes, using the following syntax:

```
class ClassName {
    -PropertyType propertyName
    +MethodName(MethodParamType methodParam) ReturnType
}
```

Classes on their own are not that useful though, so we also discussed how to show dependencies between those classes, using ..>.

Finally, we looked at some potential refactorings specific to this example. As part of that exercise, we covered how to annotate our classes using <<Annotation>>, and how one class can realize another, such as a class implementing an interface, using ..|>.

All in all, we covered a simple technique, using a class diagram, to help us write better code.

We've reached the end of the final chapter on creating diagrams. In the chapters coming up, we'll cover what to do with those diagrams once you've created them, to ensure they are useful long-term and kept up-to-date by you and your colleagues.

## CHAPTER 10

Render Diagrams Using Native Support

Up until this point, we've covered creating a variety of diagrams, using Mermaid, for a number of use cases. You're now equipped with the tools to create diagrams for everything from domain models to system designs.

However, creating those diagrams is just one half of the journey. Once you've created a diagram, how do you ensure that diagram is kept up-to-date and brings continued value from others being able to easily see it and update it?

With Streamy being off the ground and rapidly scaling up, including hiring more engineers, it's more essential than ever that new joiners can quickly get up to speed with their domain and architecture. In my experience, engineers enjoy and welcome having simple diagrams to view during onboarding. It's daunting to be presented with page after page of information when you join, but it's far less daunting to open a repository and see a diagram that you can absorb information from rapidly.

For that to become a reality, the diagrams need to be readily available and easy to update. That's what we're going to cover in this chapter: how do you integrate diagrams into your projects and daily workflows?

Leverage Native Mermaid Integrations

You can bring diagrams to life in a few ways and then easily integrate them into your day-to-day work. I'm going to start with the simplest in this chapter—using integrations for the tools you already likely use.

Firstly, we have GitHub, which has native support for Mermaid. I'm sure you've all used GitHub by now, but if not, it's the world's largest website for hosting your projects' code. It's free to create an account, and you can create unlimited public or private repositories without spending anything.

When you create a repository, you often store useful information in a project's README, or separate documentation in Markdown files. Markdown is a lightweight markup language for creating text documents, allowing you to easily create headings, lists, tables, and much more. This book is written almost exclusively in Markdown!

Render Mermaid Within Markdown Files

Throughout the book, you've been creating diagrams for a variety of use cases. They aren't going to be very useful sitting on your machine though—we want to make it easy for everyone to access them.

Since February 2022,[1] GitHub has supported Mermaid diagrams within Markdown files. All you have to do is insert the Mermaid code into the Markdown, and when the page is rendered (for example, when someone visits your project's README) it turns your Mermaid code into the rendered diagram, without any additional work from you!

Here's an example:

```
Some text that goes before your diagram.

```mermaid
flowchart LR
    A-- "test" -->B
```

Some text that goes after your diagram.
```

When viewed on GitHub, here's how it would render:

It's not just GitHub that natively supports Mermaid in Markdown though. GitLab[2] also natively supports Mermaid in its Markdown files. Other code hosting providers such as Azure DevOps, Tuleap, and Notion also natively support Mermaid.

If you ever look at Mermaid's documentation, you might notice a lot of diagrams allow you to style the diagram with CSS or add customization with JavaScript. I've deliberately not used either in this book, as in the majority

---

1. https://github.blog/2022-02-14-include-diagrams-markdown-files-mermaid/
2. https://docs.gitlab.com/ee/user/markdown.html#mermaid

of places, whether that be GitHub or in Mermaid's live editor, they're not supported. That's not to say you can't use them, but they're not necessary to unlock the power of Mermaid, and using either limits where you can easily display a diagram.

Native support is by far the easiest way to turn your Mermaid markup into an actual diagram during your day-to-day work. We can't just put the diagrams anywhere though, so let's find out where the best place to put them is.

Changing the Direction Diagrams Render In

It's worth noting some websites are thin, so you may want to change the default rendering from top-to-bottom to left-to-right, but see how it looks in the preview and then decide. Both class diagrams and flowcharts allow you to change the direction that diagrams render in. The configuration for both is as follows:

```
flowchart RL
```

```
classDiagram
    direction RL
```

This would change the direction to render right-to-left. The possible values are:

- TB: top-to-bottom
- BT: bottom-to-top
- RL: right-to-left
- LR: left-to-right

Where Should You Include Diagrams?

In terms of what diagrams I tend to put in a project, the majority of the ones we've covered are suitable. I would focus on the domain model and C4 diagrams, though, as they provide the most value at a high level and are the slowest moving of the diagrams we've looked at. It can be helpful to include high-level sequence diagrams, too, but typically I find the C4 diagrams cover that aspect well enough.

We touched a little on architecture decision records (ADRs), so if your team is using those to document decisions for a given project, inserting Mermaid diagrams into those ADRs is perfect to provide rationale for the change or explain technical flows driving the change. This is the perfect use case for sequence diagrams, to explain the flow you're working on, or perhaps an entity relationship diagram if you're making significant changes to the database.

The fun doesn't just stop with Markdown files though. On both GitHub and GitLab, you can use Mermaid anywhere Markdown is supported. For example, have you worked on a particularly complex pull request that would benefit from a visual explanation of the flow? You can include a Mermaid diagram in the pull request description! Similarly, are you struggling to explain a suggested refactor in a pull request comment? Mermaid is supported in comments too!

Unfortunately, you might be using a tool that doesn't natively support Mermaid. So let's look at how we can handle those situations as best we can.

What About Websites Without Native Support?

In a later chapter, we'll look at how we can use Mermaid's tooling to automatically turn Mermaid markup to images in Markdown files. This is another option to explore, particularly if you have an internal knowledge website that contains information on projects and has a build process you can modify.

As a last resort, you can simply export the image using one of the methods we discussed earlier in Diagramming Tools, on page xvi. Make sure you include the Mermaid markup alongside the image though. You can use `<!-- hidden content -->` in Markup to store the Mermaid markup but not actually display it. This isn't ideal, as manual work is needed to update the image, but it's better than not including the vital information at all. However, it is prone to the Mermaid markup and image being out-of-date, leading to inaccuracies.

If you can't directly use the Mermaid markup to generate the diagrams automatically and must use manual processes, you need to be extra vigilant for diagrams getting out of done. But how do you ensure they are kept up-to-date?

Keep Diagrams Up-to-Date

One of the main challenges of working with diagrams is ensuring that they are kept up-to-date. Before the introduction of Mermaid, if you wanted to include a diagram on GitHub, for example, your only option was to export the diagram you'd created as an image. Perhaps it was created using an older diagramming library, such as PlantUML. In that case, as we just discussed, you could include the image and diagram markup together.

However, a lot of diagramming tools are created using visual tools such as Visio or Diagrams.net. They save their diagrams in a format that is incomprehensible to a human, and it's certainly not reviewable, unlike Mermaid.

I've lost count of the number of times I've asked someone for the source to edit a diagram, and they inform me it was on a colleague's Google Drive, but that colleague has now left. With older diagramming libraries, and even modern UI tools for creating diagrams, the most common problem of having a static image and not being able to edit it has been resolved, thanks to Mermaid.

It's now easy to update diagrams, thanks to rendering diagrams using native tools. However, it doesn't, and cannot, solve all the problems.

Let's say you have a domain model in your project's README. As part of a piece of work, that domain model is changed—perhaps an entity is renamed or new entities added. In that case, we want to ensure the diagram detailing our domain model is updated so the domain model and code have parity. The same goes for any C4 diagrams in the project's documentation; they need to be updated as the architecture evolves.

For now, we can use a few techniques to help remind everyone to keep them up-to-date, but they're not foolproof. It does require discipline, and if you're intent on incorporating the learnings from this book into your own and your colleagues' workflows, your mindset needs to change to consider diagrams when changes are being made to a project.

That being said, you can't be expected to be solely responsible for remembering to update a diagram—that's not tenable. I've tried a few different techniques and had success with them:

1. GitHub and other tools allow you to define a pull request template. This is the default text that is populated in the pull request description when an engineer goes to open a pull request. It's relatively common to include a checklist (for example, does this PR have testing sign off? Have you bumped the version? and so on), so simply add a reminder to check for any required updates to the diagrams, and perhaps link them too.

2. As we will see in Chapter 11, Create a Static Site with Mermaid Diagrams, on page 111, a lot of code-hosting tools allow you to run automations when certain things happen. You could automatically comment on the PR, as soon as it's opened, to remind the author to update any diagram as necessary, which might be more visible than the PR description.

3. You could go one step further, and have a status check before merge that forces an engineer to confirm any documentation updates have been applied that are required. Yes, that's an extra step to merge a pull request,

but it will only take a few seconds to acknowledge in the GitHub UI, such as making a comment.

These are the techniques I've found to work so far, but implanting the importance and necessity of diagrams and documentation into your colleagues is going to be the biggest winner. If you get their buy-in, if you show them what you've learned and the power diagrams can offer, they won't need reminding. They, like you, will remember to keep these vital artifacts up-to-date. The teams I work in have become accustomed to working with diagrams and as such often reach to update or create a diagram without any nudges or reminders.

That rounds out the chapter on native support, but before we move on, it's time for you to try out the native support for yourself!

Render a Diagram on GitHub

Once again, it's your turn to try out what you learned in this chapter. This time, you won't be writing any Mermaid markup!

Instead, take one of the diagrams you created in a prior chapter and try adding it to a project on GitHub (or GitLab, if you prefer). If you don't have a GitHub account, I recommend signing up for one (it's free!) and creating a dummy project to try it out.

If the tool you use for your version control doesn't have native support, try exporting the images and adding them to a project. Remember to include the Mermaid markup alongside the rendered image!

What You've Learned

That wraps up this short chapter on displaying your Mermaid diagrams using tools with native support, such as on GitHub and GitLab. You learned that both tools, along with a few others, can take your Mermaid markup and render diagrams when they're viewed by others.

You also learned where the best places are for your diagrams—typically in the project's README or other Markdown files usually linked from the README. Finally, we covered some tips to keep your diagrams up-to-date, such as leveraging the PR description or adding automations to prompt pull request owners to update the project's documentation.

In the next chapter, we'll explore how you can generate images of your diagrams from Mermaid markup outside of relying on native support from the likes of GitHub.

## CHAPTER 11

Create a Static Site with Mermaid Diagrams

You now know we can use the power of the tools and platforms we use day-to-day to make working with Mermaid even easier. However, that only covers displaying the diagrams within a website such as GitHub, which does the work of rendering the diagrams for you. What if you want to render your Mermaid diagrams as images without relying on native tooling?

We don't want to have to convert Mermaid markup to images and update the pages manually each time we update the diagram. Wouldn't it be much better if we could do this automatically from Mermaid markup once a change is merged to the main branch?

That's exactly what we're going to cover in this chapter by deploying a Markdown file (or set of Markdown files, if you wish) to GitHub Pages on merge to the main branch. Although I chose GitHub Pages for ease of demo, you could use what we'll cover in this chapter to upload anywhere. I've converted the Markdown files to HTML and uploaded to an S3 bucket on AWS and deployed a static site containing Mermaid diagrams to Cloudflare, as other examples.

This will vary per tool, but a growing number of platforms that engineers use to house their code now support powerful automations. For example, GitHub has GitHub Actions, and GitLab has GitLab Runner. We're going to be focusing on GitHub Actions in this chapter, as the actions are incredibly simple to create, and it can be done all within GitHub's UI! You can, of course, do it in your IDE too—commit and push—but I find GitHub's UI nice to work on automations. Its UI comes with features such as syntax highlighting and direct access to the marketplace, where a range of free and paid actions already exist for you to use.

GitHub Actions, and other automation tools, are incredibly powerful. This is just one example, but the possibilities are endless. At a company I work for, we've now moved the majority of our build processes and deployments exclusively to GitHub Actions. Engineers typically enjoy working on tools such as GitHub that are made for engineers, so the more we can leverage those tools, the happier we, as engineers, will be.

Free GitHub Actions Usage

Every GitHub account comes with 2000 free minutes per month (equivalent to over 33 hours), to use with private repositories, along with 500MB of storage. If your repository is public, it's completely free to use with no limit on the number of minutes you can use. All you have to do is sign up for a GitHub account.

To host a GitHub Pages site, the repository you work on must be public or you must have a premium account. I recommend creating a brand-new public repository for the purposes of going through this action.

It's worth noting the amount of free time you receive depends on the environment you use, with Linux being by far the most economical. We'll cover how you select the environment in Learn the Basics of a GitHub Action, on page 114.

Devise a Plan of Action

Before we delve into creating an action, let's take a step back and look at what exactly we need to do to achieve our outcome. As a reminder, we want any Markdown files that are in a specific folder (in this example it will be /docs) to be uploaded to GitHub Pages, with any Mermaid markup converted to display the diagram as an image. We'll see it in action later, but Mermaid comes with a CLI that will do all of the heavy lifting for us. We can simply give the CLI a Markdown file containing Mermaid markup; it will generate SVGs from that markup and update the Markdown to reference the SVG rather than the Mermaid markup.

Here are what I believe to be the steps we need to take, and what better way to show them than in the diagram shown on page 113?

We'll go through each step in detail as we build the action, but I'll briefly touch on each one first:

1. We only want our action to trigger in certain scenarios. For our action, it's when code is pushed to the main branch (likely when a PR is merged, but you can commit straight to main too).

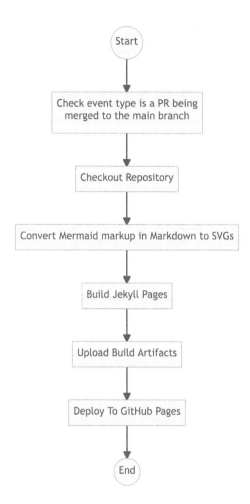

2. We can't do much without our repository, so we need to check out the repository so the action has access to it.

3. Then we need to find any Markdown files and convert any Mermaid markup in them to SVGs.

4. We'll be using Jekyll, which is a simple static site generator, to host our site on GitHub Pages. We're using this simply because GitHub has native support for Jekyll-based sites. The build step prepares the files as Jekyll expects them.

5. Penultimately, we upload the prepared build artifacts from the prior step ready to be deployed.

6. Finally, we use the uploaded build artifacts to deploy them to our GitHub pages site.

If you're not familiar with GitHub Actions, or GitHub Pages, it may not be immediately obvious how to do any of these steps. Don't worry, though; it'll be much simpler than it sounds, and we won't even need to write much actual code to achieve it!

You may have noticed that the preceding diagram is a very simple flowchart, of course created using Mermaid. This is a throwaway diagram, in that it's just to visualize the steps I needed to take. Not all diagrams have to be a work of art or be complex. Sometimes it can help to just take a step back and visualize what it is you need to do.

Learn the Basics of a GitHub Action

Ready? Let's get started!

As opposed to other chapters where you completed an exercise at the end, this time treat this as a step-by-step tutorial to creating your first GitHub Action. As I take you through the steps, follow along using your own GitHub account.

First, we need to create a brand-new action. GitHub makes this super-simple; you go to a repository (or create a new one—remember it has to be public!), click the Actions tab at the top, click the new workflow button, and finally select Simple Workflow. Each action you create can be thought of as a work-flow, a series of steps to take to complete a given task.

You should now have something like the following:

```
# This is a basic workflow to help you get started with Actions
name: CI

# Controls when the workflow will run
on:
  # Triggers the workflow on push or pull request events
  # but only for the "main" branch
  push:
    branches: [ "main" ]
  pull_request:
    branches: [ "main" ]

  # Allows you to run this workflow manually from the Actions tab
  workflow_dispatch:
```

```
# A workflow run is made up of one or more jobs
# that can run sequentially or in parallel
jobs:
  # This workflow contains a single job called "build"
  build:
    # The type of runner that the job will run on
    runs-on: ubuntu-latest

    # Steps represent a sequence of tasks that
    # will be executed as part of the job
    steps:
      # Checks-out your repository
      # so your job can access it
      - uses: actions/checkout@v3

      # Runs a single command using the runners shell
      - name: Run a one-line script
        run: echo Hello, world!

      # Runs a set of commands using the runners shell
      - name: Run a multi-line script
        run: |
          echo Add other actions to build,
          echo test, and deploy your project.
```

This is the basic structure for any GitHub Action and comes full of helpful comments. For anyone not familiar, the configuration is defined using YAML, which is a human-friendly data serialization format.

I'll add a little more information to some of the sections, starting with controlling when the workflow will run. This is defined by this section:

```
on:
  # Triggers the workflow on push or pull request events
  # but only for the "main" branch
  push:
    branches: [ "main" ]
  pull_request:
    branches: [ "main" ]
```

Under on, we can list any number of GitHub Events[1] to trigger an action. In this case, it will trigger when code is pushed and when anything happens to a pull request (for example, opened or closed, but there are many more). We can further refine, for each event, when to trigger an action. In this example, the action will only get triggered on the "main" branch. GitHub's documentation contains all the possible events and the filter options for each event.

---

1. https://docs.github.com/en/actions/using-workflows/events-that-trigger-workflows

Next, we define the jobs we want to run for this action and what operating system to run them on:

```
# A workflow run is made up of one or more jobs
# that can run sequentially or in parallel
jobs:
  # This workflow contains a single job called "build"
  build:
    # The type of runner that the job will run on
    runs-on: ubuntu-latest
```

Under jobs, you can list as many jobs as you like. In the example action, there's just one—build, which runs on Ubuntu. Other operating systems are available,[2] including Windows and Mac, but they're more expensive. You could run all your actions with a single job, but there are efficiency gains from defining multiple and parallelizing the jobs where possible, as any number of jobs can run in a single workflow in parallel.

A classic example of this would be deployments. We might want to run our test suite and at the same time build the Docker container ready for deployment. We could do them sequentially, but it would be a lot faster to run them in parallel. Similarly, if we're deploying multiple elements, for example a web app and a Kafka consumer, we can possibly do so in parallel.

Finally, each job can have any number of steps to complete that job, as shown in the example:

```
# Steps represent a sequence of tasks that
# will be executed as part of the job
steps:
  # Checks-out your repository
  # so your job can access it
  - uses: actions/checkout@v3

  # Runs a single command using the runners shell
  - name: Run a one-line script
    run: echo Hello, world!
```

Unlike jobs, steps cannot run in parallel at this time and always run sequentially. Each step can run commands, same as you would in your terminal, or leverage another GitHub Action to run. GitHub itself provides many actions for you to use. In our first step we're using their checkout action, which checks out the repository's code, so that our action has access to the codebase. In the second step, it simply outputs some text by executing code

---

2. https://docs.github.com/en/actions/using-github-hosted-runners/about-github-hosted-runners#supported-runners-and-hardware-resources

against the runner's shell. GitHub's documentation[3] is extensive and can explain every possible workflow configuration option. I've covered the basics we'll need.

Start by Defining the Events That Trigger the Action

Now that you understand what GitHub Actions are, and how they can be created, you can start editing the simple workflow to implement the flow we looked at in Devise a Plan of Action, on page 112. We'll build upon the default workflow GitHub provides to us.

To begin with, we're going to update the name to reflect our action and modify the events we care about slightly. The event we care about is when a commit is pushed to the main branch. So we update name and on to look like so:

```
name: Convert And Deploy Mermaid Diagrams In Markdown To GitHub Pages

# Runs on pushes targeting the default branch
on:
  push:
    branches: ["main"]

# Sets permissions of the GITHUB_TOKEN to allow deployment to GitHub Pages
permissions:
  contents: read
  pages: write
  id-token: write
```

You can list any number of events to trigger the action, but we just care about one case. We've also added another section, permissions, that defines what permissions the GitHub Action can take. In this case, we need to specify some additional permissions, particularly the pages and id-token ones, which allow our action to write to GitHub Pages. Typically, you don't need to adjust permissions—it's just for this particular use case we need permissions to access pages. If you're using an action from the marketplace, the documentation should tell you if you need to set any additional permissions.

Now that our action will trigger when we need it to, we can start crafting the actual logic for our action.

Check Out the Repository's Code

We've defined when to run the action, but not the actual logic the action needs to execute. We'll be splitting our action into two jobs, as we have two distinct

---

3. https://docs.github.com/en/actions/using-workflows/workflow-syntax-for-github-actions

phases: build and deploy. For now, we're going to work on the build step of our action, which has a number of steps. I'll add the steps in batches and explain what each one is doing.

You can remove anything under jobs and replace it with the following:

```
# A workflow run is made up of one or more jobs
# that can run sequentially or in parallel
jobs:
  # Build job
  build:
    # The type of runner that the job will run on
    runs-on: ubuntu-latest
    # Steps represent a sequence of tasks that
    # will be executed as part of the job
    steps:
      - name: Checkout
        uses: actions/checkout@v3
```

Here, we've added one job, to be run on Ubuntu, and added the first step, which is simply checking out the repository's code into the runner that executes the action.

Now we can start adding our action-specific logic. As per the flowchart, we must first convert any Mermaid markup in Markdown files to SVGs. Let's look at how we can do that!

Convert Mermaid Markup to SVGs in Markdown

Now that we have the code from our repository checked out, we need to find any Markdown files in the docs directory and use Mermaid's CLI to convert any Mermaid markup in them to SVGs. This is because, by default, GitHub Pages won't render Mermaid markup as an image like it does in Markdown files in your code's repository.

Instead of using uses to specify an action to use, we instead use run to supply the code to execute. As we're running on Linux, this is Bash code:

```
- name: Generate Diagrams In Markdown Files
  run: |
    cd docs
    for file in $(find . -name '*.md'); do
      [ -f "$file" ] || continue
      npx -p @mermaid-js/mermaid-cli mmdc --input $file --output $file
    done
```

We're choosing to write a little bit of code ourselves here, as there isn't an action that can do it for us like when we checked out the repository. Three main steps are happening here:

1. We change directory to the docs directory, as that's the directory we want to deploy to GitHub Pages. You could use another directory, or remove the line to deploy everything in the root (and its subdirectories).

2. Next, we use a loop to iterate over every file ending in .md. We use find, which will recursively search for the pattern specified. So if you have sub-directories, it will find the files in there too.

3. Finally, we use the Mermaid CLI to convert any Mermaid markup to SVGs. We do this by supplying the input and output as the file we wish to convert. It's safe to run on Markdown files without Mermaid too—the CLI will ignore those. We're using npx, which is a quick and easy way to run NPM packages without having to install them.

If you want to see all the capabilities of Mermaid's CLI, you can run npx -p @mermaid-js/mermaid-cli mmdc -h locally or read through the documentation.[4]

If we were to run our action now, we'd see our Markdown files being converted to contain SVGs in place of Mermaid markup in the logs. Next, we need to upload these prepared Markdown files to GitHub Pages, which takes several more steps to achieve. Let's look at how we can prepare our Markdown files for GitHub Pages.

Build Jekyll Artifacts

Unfortunately, we can't upload Markdown files straight to GitHub Pages. It needs the files to be prepared in a certain way, such as converted to HTML, along with some configuration. Luckily for us, we don't need to know the ins and outs of preparing the files, as we can delegate that responsibility to open source actions!

We don't have to always write the logic ourselves. A wide range of open source actions is available to us to use for free inside our action. These are like small libraries, similar to libraries provided by package managers in most modern programming languages.

That's what we'll use for the remainder of the steps in this action. We'll leverage actions provided by GitHub, as deploying a site to GitHub Pages isn't

---

4. https://github.com/mermaid-js/mermaid-cli

trivial. Here's how to prepare the Markdown files to be uploaded to GitHub pages:

```
- name: Setup Pages
  uses: actions/configure-pages@v2
- name: Build with Jekyll
  uses: actions/jekyll-build-pages@v1
  with:
    source: ./docs
    destination: ./_site
- name: Upload artifact
  uses: actions/upload-pages-artifact@v1
```

We're adding three steps, each using a different action. The first enables Pages and extracts some metadata about the site we wish to create. The second prepares the contents of docs, as Jekyll requires HTML files and places the files in /_site. The third uploads the artifacts ready to be deployed to GitHub pages.

Using with in conjunction with an action allows us to pass parameters to that action. In this case, we're specfiying the source (in our case, the docs directory) and the destination. You could specify any source and destination you wish. If you chose to build the artifacts and not place them in /_site, we could use with when uploading to specify the directory. By default, upload-pages-artifact will upload anything in /_site, so we can omit the with parameter for that action.

We're seeing the real power of GitHub Actions here. I've never used Jekyll, nor have I regularly used GitHub Pages, but using open source actions, I don't need to know how to use either, as the actions are doing all the heavy lifting for me with a few lines of configuration, and all for free.

We're almost finished—now that we've prepared everything for GitHub Pages, we can deploy it to make our changes live!

Deploy to GitHub Pages

Everything should now be prepared for GitHub Pages. All that's left to do is deploy to GitHub Pages. Once again, we can lean on an open source action provided by GitHub to do this work for us. We'll add the second job now, so after the preceding build job is completed, it will move on to the deploy job.

You could run the deploy as another step inside the build job, but I want to show you how you can define multiple jobs and how that reflects on GitHub's UI.

```
# Deployment job
deploy:
```

```
  environment:
    name: github-pages
    url: ${{ steps.deployment.outputs.page_url }}
  runs-on: ubuntu-latest
  needs: build
  steps:
    - name: Deploy to GitHub Pages
      id: deployment
      uses: actions/deploy-pages@v1
```

Simple, right? That's all that's needed to create a site on GitHub Pages. We have a couple of new pieces of configuration here, so let's look at those quickly:

1. We specify environment under the deployment job. This is exactly as it sounds and sets the environment that the action executes in. GitHub itself recommends github-pages for this action, but you can create your own for other actions. For example, it's common to have staging and production when deploying applications. We can also set a URL for that environment—in this case we're using the output from the deployment step further down. When the action runs, and completes, it will show that URL on the deployment step in the GitHub UI, which we'll see shortly when we run our action. Environments are powerful—for example, you can control what branches can deploy to a specific environment (for instance, limit production to main so that feature branches aren't accidentally deployed to production).

2. By default, jobs will execute in parallel. That's where needs is required, as we can specify the jobs that are required to successfully complete before this job starts. In this case, we want the build to complete before we run deploy.

Although we haven't needed it much in our workflow, using outputs from steps is incredibly useful. We use it in the preceding step to set the url of the environment, and it uses the format ${{ steps.NAME-OF-STEP.outputs.NAME-OF-OUTPUT-VAR }}.

Any actions that provide output will likely document the output. An action I've used previously allows you to detect what files were changed for a given commit, and once that action has run, it provides the output for you to use as per the preceding description. For example, you can retrieve the list of files changed in that commit.

That's the last step—we can now try running the action and deploying to GitHub Pages!

Run the Action

All the work to set up the action is now done, and we can commit it to our repository into the main branch. If you used the new workflow button, GitHub will have created the file in the right location for you. However, just in case, it needs to be saved in .github/workflows/your-action-name.yml. Here's the full action, combining all the preceding steps:

```
name: Convert And Deploy Mermaid Diagrams In Markdown

# Runs on pushes targeting the default branch
on:
  push:
    branches: ["main"]

# Sets permissions of the GITHUB_TOKEN to allow deployment to GitHub Pages
permissions:
  contents: read
  pages: write
  id-token: write

# A workflow run is made up of one or more jobs
# that can run sequentially or in parallel
jobs:
  # Build job
  build:
    # The type of runner that the job will run on
    runs-on: ubuntu-latest
    # Steps represent a sequence of tasks that
    # will be executed as part of the job
    steps:
      - name: Checkout
        uses: actions/checkout@v3
        # Generate Images In Markdown Files
      - name: Generate Diagrams In Markdown Files
        run: |
          cd docs
          for file in $(find . -name '*.md'); do
            [ -f "$file" ] || continue
            npx -p @mermaid-js/mermaid-cli mmdc --input $file --output $file
          done
      - name: Setup Pages
        uses: actions/configure-pages@v2
      - name: Build with Jekyll
        uses: actions/jekyll-build-pages@v1
        with:
          source: ./docs
          destination: ./_site
      - name: Upload artifact
        uses: actions/upload-pages-artifact@v1
```

```
# Deployment job
deploy:
  environment:
    name: github-pages
    url: ${{ steps.deployment.outputs.page_url }}
  runs-on: ubuntu-latest
  needs: build
  steps:
    - name: Test
      run: echo
    - name: Deploy to GitHub Pages
      id: deployment
      uses: actions/deploy-pages@v1
```

The last thing we need to do is create a Markdown file in the /docs folder, containing Mermaid markup, and commit that, too, so the action has something to work with. We can see all the actions that run under the Actions tab on the repository's page, and there will be a list of all the workflows that have run previously. If you click the top one, and wait for it to finish, you'll see something like this:

I find the UI useful and full of information. For example, we can see who triggered the workflow, the status, and how long the action took to execute. We can see at a glance the jobs that executed—in our case it's build and deploy—and we can also see any artifacts that were produced. In this case, there's one artifact, which was created during the upload-pages-artifact action. You can click that artifact and download it to see how the files were prepared for Jekyll if you're curious.

If you want more fine-grained information on a job, that's available to you too. If you click a job, such as build, it will take you into that job and show you the steps completed for that job. This is useful for debugging, as you can expand each step to see the log output for that step.

Finally, you can see the environment URL working on the deploy step. It will output the URL for your newly created pages site. If you click it, you'll see your pages site. I called my Markdown file test, so once I click the URL, I can add /test to the URL to see my generated page. Similarly to static HTML, you can create an index.md file that will render in the root of any directory (for example, /docs/index.md would render on the root of your GitHub Pages site).

That's it! You've successfully deployed to GitHub Pages and transformed any Mermaid markup to a rendered image, making updating those diagrams a breeze for anyone in future, without any manual work to regenerate the images. This allows you and your colleagues to easily add diagrams to your content pages hosted outside of GitHub, perhaps on your blog, for example, or knowledge articles used internally. That's exactly what we do at a company I work for—we have an internally hosted knowledge site, accessible by the entire business (as not everyone has access to GitHub).

Render Diagrams on Page Load

In this chapter, we've covered how we can automatically convert Mermaid markup in Markdown into rendered diagrams. This is definitely the best way, in my opinion, to handle the conversion. However, you can use Mermaid's JavaScript API[5] directly in your pages, if you wish, as an alternative.

What You've Learned

We covered a lot in this chapter, but I can't overstate the power of tools such as GitHub Actions. Lately, in my experience, more and more tasks are moving to automated tools directly in the code hosting tools we all use day after day. This book is about diagrams rather than GitHub Actions, but it's important to modernize processes such as diagramming with the latest automation tools to unlock the power of diagramming.

This is where Mermaid really shines, with modern tooling, native support and integrations, and endless possibilities. In this chapter, we went over a simple automation, but there are other things to try. For example, in a world of distributed systems, and lots of repositories, the domain model of a given company is spread out amongst those distributed services, each one responsible for a part of the domain model and likely each documenting its part of the domain model. What if you automated the creation of a company-wide domain model by combining the domain models in each repository,

---

5.   https://mermaid-js.github.io/mermaid/#/n00b-gettingStarted?id=_3-calling-the-javascript-api

rather than either lacking that information, or attempting to keep a company-wide domain model up-to-date manually?

You've learned the basic format for any GitHub Action, using on to define the types of events that should trigger the action, along with any event-specific filtering to apply, such as specific branch names. Next, we covered how to define jobs, which are GitHub Action's mechanism to parallelize different parts of your workflow or even just break it up into logic parts. In our case, we defined two jobs and covered how to make one job dependent on another job's completion before it starts its work.

Finally, you learned to define steps within a job. A job can contain an unlimited number of steps, either leveraging existing GitHub Actions created by others or by executing code against the GitHub runner's shell.

Putting it all together, you learned how to convert Mermaid markup in Markdown files to contain SVGs instead and deploy the converted Markdown files to a GitHub Pages site.

## CHAPTER 12

What You've Learned

Congratulations! You've reached the end of your journey on learning about technical diagramming and Mermaid. Or have you? In my opinion, this is just the beginning. I've given you the tools and techniques needed to succeed when it comes to advancing and improving your career using diagrams. However, the onus is now on you to take these learnings, to master what you've learned, and share what you've learned with others. Being able to diagram will serve you well as an individual, but it's going to be so much more powerful if you can bring others along with you.

Whether that's collaborating on a domain model with your colleagues, presenting a proposal for a system's architecture to senior leadership, or helping a new joiner understand how an application flows, each time you introduce someone to diagramming, you not only learn more yourself, you enhance their learning and careers too. A number of my colleagues had never diagrammed before I introduced it to them, and now they often produce diagrams without so much as a nudge from me—because they can truly see the value that a diagram can bring.

It might take a little while for you to win some people over—after all they may have been burned by the likes of manual drawing tools, stuck in them for hours lining up boxes and lines. Mermaid removes all that pain, though, with its easy-to-use markup and automatic rendering. It's rare I recommend Mermaid to someone and they don't instantly enjoy using it and see the benefit in it.

Although a lot of the book was about Mermaid, the diagrams themselves are what's important. Mermaid is just a tool, and tools come and go. I think Mermaid will be around for the forseeable, but should a new tool emerge, everything you learned about diagramming is still incredibly relevant. As long as the tool allows you to easily update a diagram, doesn't have manual exports of images, and is diffable, it will be a perfectly fine tool to use. As you learned, though, Mermaid is currently the clear winner because of its widespread adoption, most of all within the tools you already likely use, such as GitHub and GitLab.

I hope you've enjoyed this book and, most importantly, have lots of takeaways from it to apply to your day-to-day work. Unlike a book on a programming language, you don't need a project to start using what you've learned right away. Hopefully you've completed the exercises as you've gone through the book, or plan to go back and complete them, as there's nothing better for cementing knowledge than practicing what you've learned. When I was first learning to diagram, I found excuses to do so in my day-to-day work. The chances are, during the course of reading this book, you've had multiple opportunities to diagram. Now you just need to take the time to crystalize what you've learned.

If you want to chat about anything in the book, or have any questions, don't hesitate to reach out to me via any of the following:

- Email: ashley@technicalbookclub.com
- Twitter: @_ashleypeacock

Bibliography

[Eva03]   Eric Evans. *Domain-Driven Design: Tackling Complexity in the Heart of Software*. Addison-Wesley Longman, Boston, MA, First, 2003.

Thank you!

We hope you enjoyed this book and that you're already thinking about what you want to learn next. To help make that decision easier, we're offering you this gift.

Head over to https://pragprog.com right now and use the coupon code BUYAN-OTHER2023 to save 30% on your next ebook. Void where prohibited or restricted. This offer does not apply to any edition of the *The Pragmatic Programmer* ebook.

And if you'd like to share your own expertise with the world, why not propose a writing idea to us? After all, many of our best authors started off as our readers, just like you. With a 50% royalty, world-class editorial services, and a name you trust, there's nothing to lose. Visit https://pragprog.com/become-an-author/ today to learn more and to get started.

We thank you for your continued support, and we hope to hear from you again soon!

The Pragmatic Bookshelf

Domain Modeling Made Functional

You want increased customer satisfaction, faster development cycles, and less wasted work. Domain-driven design (DDD) combined with functional programming is the innovative combo that will get you there. In this pragmatic, down-to-earth guide, you'll see how applying the core principles of functional programming can result in software designs that model real-world requirements both elegantly and concisely—often more so than an object-oriented approach. Practical examples in the open-source F# functional language, and examples from familiar business domains, show you how to apply these techniques to build software that is business-focused, flexible, and high quality.

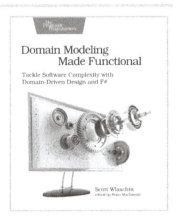

Scott Wlaschin
(310 pages) ISBN: 9781680502541. $47.95
https://pragprog.com/book/swdddf

Design It!

Don't engineer by coincidence—design it like you mean it! Grounded by fundamentals and filled with practical design methods, this is the perfect introduction to software architecture for programmers who are ready to grow their design skills. Ask the right stakeholders the right questions, explore design options, share your design decisions, and facilitate collaborative workshops that are fast, effective, and fun. Become a better programmer, leader, and designer. Use your new skills to lead your team in implementing software with the right capabilities—and develop awesome software!

Michael Keeling
(358 pages) ISBN: 9781680502091. $41.95
https://pragprog.com/book/mkdsa

Designing Data Governance from the Ground Up

Businesses own more data than ever before, but it's of no value if you don't know how to use it. Data governance manages the people, processes, and strategy needed for deploying data projects to production. But doing it well is far from easy: Less than one fourth of business leaders say their organizations are data driven. In *Designing Data Governance from the Ground Up*, you'll build a cross-functional strategy to create roadmaps and stewardship for data-focused projects, embed data governance into your engineering practice, and put processes in place to monitor data after deployment.

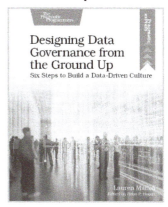

Lauren Maffeo
(100 pages) ISBN: 9781680509809. $29.95
https://pragprog.com/book/lmmlops

Numerical Brain Teasers

Challenge your brain with math! Using nothing more than basic arithmetic and logic, you'll be thrilled as answers slot into place. Whether purely for fun or to test your knowledge, you'll sharpen your problem-solving skills and flex your mental muscles. All you need is logical thought, a little patience, and a clear mind. There are no gotchas here. These puzzles are the perfect introduction to or refresher for math concepts you may have only just learned or long since forgotten. Get ready to have more fun with numbers than you've ever had before.

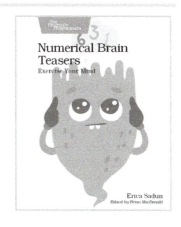

Erica Sadun
(186 pages) ISBN: 9781680509748. $18.95
https://pragprog.com/book/esbrain

Modern Front-End Development for Rails, Second Edition

Improve the user experience for your Rails app with rich, engaging client-side interactions. Learn to use the Rails 7 tools and simplify the complex JavaScript ecosystem. It's easier than ever to build user interactions with Hotwire, Turbo, and Stimulus. You can add great front-end flair without much extra complication. Use React to build a more complex set of client-side features. Structure your code for different levels of client-side needs with these powerful options. Add to your toolkit today!

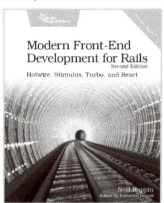

Noel Rappin
(408 pages) ISBN: 9781680509618. $55.95
https://pragprog.com/book/nrclient2

Exploring Graphs with Elixir

Data is everywhere—it's just not very well connected, which makes it super hard to relate dataset to dataset. Using graphs as the underlying glue, you can readily join data together and create navigation paths across diverse sets of data. Add Elixir, with its awesome power of concurrency, and you'll soon be mastering data networks. Learn how different graph models can be accessed and used from within Elixir and how you can build a robust semantics overlay on top of graph data structures. We'll start from the basics and examine the main graph paradigms. Get ready to embrace the world of connected data!

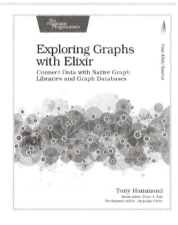

Tony Hammond
(294 pages) ISBN: 9781680508406. $47.95
https://pragprog.com/book/thgraphs

SQL Antipatterns, Volume 1

SQL is the ubiquitous language for software developers working with structured data. Most developers who rely on SQL are experts in their favorite language (such as Java, Python, or Go), but they're not experts in SQL. They often depend on antipatterns—solutions that look right but become increasingly painful to work with as you uncover their hidden costs. Learn to identify and avoid many of these common blunders. Refactor an inherited nightmare into a data model that really works. Updated for the current versions of MySQL and Python, this new edition adds a dozen brand new mini-antipatterns for quick wins.

Bill Karwin
(378 pages) ISBN: 9781680508987. $47.95
https://pragprog.com/book/bksap1

Build Talking Apps for Alexa

Voice recognition is here at last. Alexa and other voice assistants have now become widespread and mainstream. Is your app ready for voice interaction? Learn how to develop your own voice applications for Amazon Alexa. Start with techniques for building conversational user interfaces and dialog management. Integrate with existing applications and visual interfaces to complement voice-first applications. The future of human-computer interaction is voice, and we'll help you get ready for it.

Craig Walls
(388 pages) ISBN: 9781680507256. $47.95
https://pragprog.com/book/cwalexa

The Pragmatic Bookshelf

The Pragmatic Bookshelf features books written by professional developers for professional developers. The titles continue the well-known Pragmatic Programmer style and continue to garner awards and rave reviews. As development gets more and more difficult, the Pragmatic Programmers will be there with more titles and products to help you stay on top of your game.

Visit Us Online

This Book's Home Page
https://pragprog.com/book/apdiag
Source code from this book, errata, and other resources. Come give us feedback, too!

Keep Up-to-Date
https://pragprog.com
Join our announcement mailing list (low volume) or follow us on Twitter @pragprog for new titles, sales, coupons, hot tips, and more.

New and Noteworthy
https://pragprog.com/news
Check out the latest Pragmatic developments, new titles, and other offerings.

Save on the ebook

Save on the ebook versions of this title. Owning the paper version of this book entitles you to purchase the electronic versions at a terrific discount.

PDFs are great for carrying around on your laptop—they are hyperlinked, have color, and are fully searchable. Most titles are also available for the iPhone and iPod touch, Amazon Kindle, and other popular e-book readers.

Send a copy of your receipt to support@pragprog.com and we'll provide you with a discount coupon.

Contact Us

Online Orders:	*https://pragprog.com/catalog*
Customer Service:	*support@pragprog.com*
International Rights:	*translations@pragprog.com*
Academic Use:	*academic@pragprog.com*
Write for Us:	*http://write-for-us.pragprog.com*
Or Call:	+1 800-699-7764

Lightning Source UK Ltd.
Milton Keynes UK
UKHW032008220223
417472UK00003B/3